Sentinel of Service Protecting Durham - The Bull City

Policing's Evolution Nationally and Locally - Preserving the Legacy of the Historic Hayti District

TONY L. SCOTT

ISBN: 979-8-9885933-7-9 (Paperback)
ISBN: 979-8-9885933-8-6 (Hardback)

For more information or permissions, please contact the author:
redeemedwriter718@gmail.com
tlmdscott2@gmail.com

Editor: This book was self-edited by the author.

Cover Design/Book Project Management:
Raindrop Creative, Inc. | StartWrite Publish Team
http://www.raindropbrand.com

DEDICATION

To my lovely wife, Lisa Land Scott,
Your unwavering love and support as a Christian spouse have been the cornerstone of my life. During my nearly three decades of service as a Law Enforcement Officer and beyond, you stood by me as my greatest supporter. I am forever grateful for your continuous prayers and the selfless way you cared for our sons while I was on duty. This book would not have been possible without your support and devotion as a caring and loving mother and wife!

To my sons, Desmond and Mario,
You were my pride and joy, and your lives as little ones under my care inspired me to strive to do my best for you as your father and protector. I now look at you two as men, husbands and fathers, and I'm so proud of your accomplishments!

To my grandson, Harrison, and my granddaughter, Rumi,
You are growing up in a world where law enforcement does not hold the same respect it once did. My prayer is that you will come to honor and appreciate those who dedicate their lives to serving and protecting others.

This book is for all of you. It stands as a testament to the values of resilience, service and love that have guided me throughout my life's journey.

Table of Contents

Preface 1

Introduction 3

Chapter 1 History Of Policing In Durham: The Hayti 5
Community, & Policing in North America

Chapter 2 A New Beginning, A Hard Road: From Soldier to 33
Sentinel

Chapter 3 District 1 – High Hopes & A Hell of a Ride! 53

Chapter 4 A Rising Sentinel: The Go-Getter, but Hold on a 73
Minute

Chapter 5 Sleepeth No More: Growth & Change Within the 83
Bull City

Chapter 6 A Sentinel to District 4 & Beyond 93

Chapter 7 Specialized Work Assignments: C.A.T.T. & S.E.T. 127

Chapter 8 Specialized Work Assignment: Selective Enforcement 165
Tactical Team (S.E.T.T.)

Chapter 9 Detective T.L. Scott 195

Chapter 10 Community Oriented Policing (C.O.P.), Gang 205
Resistance Education And Training (G.R.E.A.T.),
The Last of My Assignments

Chapter 11 Defund the Police – What Foolishness 217

Preface

D urham, North Carolina – known proudly as *The Bull City* – is more than just a place on the map. For me, it is home. Born and raised in this vibrant community, Durham *(The Old Hayti District)*, in some ways, has helped shape who I am and given me the foundation to pursue a life of service. From my early years in this city to my career protecting its streets, Durham's unique character has been the backdrop to my personal and professional journey.

Sentinel of Service: Protecting Durham, The Bull City is a deeply personal account of my transition from serving as a *Soldier* to becoming a *Law Enforcement Officer* and, ultimately, to retirement. Over the years, I have served my hometown in many capacities: as a uniform patrol officer, a member of specialized units, the Crime Area Target Team and Selective Enforcement Tactical Team, a Detective, a mentor in schools through the Gang Resistance Education and Training program, a Community Oriented Policing Officer, and lastly, a desk officer. Each role has allowed me to serve my community, for which I'm grateful to have been able to make a difference as a positive influencer.

In addition to recounting my personal experiences, this book explores the broader context of policing. I provide a brief history of policing in the United States, offering insights into its evolution and the challenges that have shaped the profession over the years. I also delve into the history of the Durham Police Department, highlighting its role in protecting and serving a city as dynamic as Durham. Additionally, helping to preserve the history of *The Old Hayti District – Blackwall Street*, with this community's first African American Police Officers.

Through this book, I aim to share the lessons, challenges, and triumphs that marked my career while placing them within the larger story of real-life law enforcement and not that which is viewed on television. My hope is that my story resonates with anyone who has ever felt the pull of service, the pride of community, or the weight of responsibility of protecting and serving the community you took an oath to serve.

This is my story, with my roots in Durham – *The Old Hayti District*, and I'm honored to share it with you.

Introduction

Durham, North Carolina – *The Bull City* – has always been a part of me. Born and raised in this community, I've seen it grow, change, and evolve over the years. It is here that I learned the values of hard work, resilience, and connection, and it is here that I answered the call to serve – first as a *Soldier*, then as a *Law Enforcement Officer*.

*["The Bull City" is tied to the **Bull** brand of tobacco products that were produced in Durham].*

This book, **Sentinel of Service: Protecting Durham, The Bull City**, is a reflection of my life's journey, from growing up in Durham to dedicating my career to protecting it. My time in the military instilled in me the discipline, perseverance, and teamwork that laid the foundation for my transition to law enforcement. Over the years, I'd served in various capacities. Each of these roles gave me a unique perspective on the city and its people, along with the challenges of policing from without and from within the DPD.

In addition to sharing my personal journey, this book provides a broader context for understanding law enforcement. I offer a brief history of policing in the United States, tracing its origins and evolution into the profession it is today. I also explore the history of the Durham Police

Department, highlighting its unique role in shaping and protecting this vibrant city through its hiring of its first and pioneering African American Officers, who patrolled the **Historic "Black" Hayti District**. These historical perspectives provide a backdrop for my own experiences and help to frame the larger story of public service.

This is not a book about policing in general or the collective stories of others in law enforcement. It is my story – what it meant to serve the community I grew up in, to protect the streets I once walked as a child, and my experience within the law enforcement community. Through my years of service, I came to understand the true meaning of *Community Policing* and the deep connection between a *Sentinel* and their community.

Durham is more than just my hometown; it is a place where I was able to positively impact the lives of many as a *Law Enforcement Officer!* I hope that as you read this book, you'll gain a deeper appreciation for the challenges and rewards of serving one's community and, assuredly, see a bit of Durham's story through my eyes.

Whether you are a native of *The Bull City*, a fellow officer, or simply someone curious about the life of service, I welcome you to take *A Ride-along* with me. This is the story of a *Soldier* turned *Sentinel*, of protecting the place I've always called home. You don't have to sign a waiver for my *Ride Ride-along Program*.

However, wearing your seat belt – *It's the Law. Buckle up!*

CHAPTER I

History Of Policing In Durham: The Hayti Community, & Policing in North America

My Brief History and Encounter with Policing in My Community

As a young man in my early 30s, with adolescent sons to consider, I began for the first time to give thought to *Race in America*. Very little, if any, public school curriculums gave adequate attention to African American History in this country. Among the many things that stood out to me, I was struck to silence when I realized I was born during the *Civil Rights Era*. I remember thinking and surprisingly grasping that the African American fight for justice and equality was a mere three decades earlier!

And that many who are unapologetically racist to their core were in positions of power and influence! Then there are those who have racist tendencies who are oblivious to this fact. While there are countless others, as I had been, who are clueless to the reality that *Jim Crow Laws*, segregation and such practices, knowingly or not, are in place that promote *Systemic Racism*. And so, the struggle continues!

Race Relations within America's Ethnicities – this "melting pot," particularly in the context of African Americans, has historically been viewed with suspicion and negativity, shaped by centuries of racial prejudice and systemic inequality. In many instances, this perception has translated into unjust treatment and discrimination, often embedded within societal institutions like law enforcement. Growing up as an African American in Durham, North Carolina, with my early years – from birth to 6 years of age being within the Historic "Black" Hayti District that was being taken over by *Urban Renewal* or *Gentrification* – I call this "White Might." I was not much older than 6 years of age when I knowingly encountered firsthand an experience that shed some light on these racial tensions.

As a young boy attending Merrick Moore Elementary School, I vividly remember playing on a pile of wooden pallets behind a local business (Canada Dry) when a white police officer arrived and placed another child and me in the back of his car. My family lived in Cheek Rd Apartments not far from this business that was located on Hardee's Street. Another officer soon joined, dismissively the officer who placed me in his police car referred to us as "these two nigger boys." That encounter, though brief, left a lasting impression of how I, as an African American child, was perceived with disdain and suspicion simply for ***Playing While "Black."***

In a separate situation, when my parents were not home, a white police officer arrived at our apartment, and despite my mother's strict instructions not to open the door for *anyone*, I was intimidated by him into doing so! My fear of the presence of this white officer in my home and his interaction with me further underscored the racial power imbalance.

Additionally, I recall my father discussing with my mother an encounter where a white officer harassed him for driving without shoes – today, we call this ***Driving While Black*** or racial profiling. These early experiences were compounded by a later interaction as an adult working in law enforcement. I am now a 10 to 15-year veteran of the Durham Police Department. I was relaxing and enjoying the day while lying back on a picnic table in a local park in my community when a white officer approached me.

He exits his vehicle, and as he approaches me, he takes out his nightstick. After an exchange of a few words, one of which was, "Why do you have your nightstick in your hand." It was only after I identified myself as a fellow officer did the situation somewhat de-escalated. These moments highlight the way African Americans are often viewed through a lens of suspicion, fear, and even hostility, a reality shaped by historical inequalities and racial profiling, a pattern that continues to affect interactions between law enforcement and "Black" communities.

The history of policing in Durham, North Carolina, is marked by its development alongside the city's growth, particularly in relation to race, labor, and civil rights. Durham has a rich history as a center of industry, education, and African American culture, and its police department reflects the city's complex history, especially in relation to racial dynamics.

Early History (Late 1800s - Early 1900s)

- **Pre-Police Days**: In the late 19th century, Durham was a growing town in North Carolina, fueled by tobacco and textile industries. Policing in the area before formal police departments was largely carried out by local lawmen, constables, and watchmen. These individuals had limited authority and were primarily responsible for maintaining order in a rapidly growing urban environment.

- **Formation of Durham Police Department**: As Durham's population and economic importance grew, the need for a more organized law enforcement system became evident. In 1887, the **Durham Police Department (DPD)** was officially established, marking the beginning of formal policing in the city. At that time, Durham was also experiencing a boom in tobacco manufacturing, which brought in large numbers of laborers, many of whom were African American.

Racial Tensions and the Early 20th Century (1900s - 1940s)

- **Jim Crow Era**: Like much of the South, Durham during the early 20th century was deeply segregated due to **Jim Crow laws** that enforced racial discrimination. The police department was often involved in maintaining the status quo of racial segregation, including policing African American communities, enforcing curfews, and responding to labor strikes or civil disobedience.

- **Police and the "Black" Community**: African Americans in Durham, particularly those who were involved in the tobacco industry, played a crucial role in the city's economy. However, they were often subjected to discriminatory practices, including unequal treatment by the police. During this time, police forces in Durham, as elsewhere in the South, were frequently seen as instruments of racial control and oppression, targeting "Black" communities with heightened surveillance and brutal tactics.

- **The Role of Policing in Labor Unrest**: As Durham's economy grew, the city saw significant labor unrest, particularly in the tobacco factories. The police often played a role in quelling strikes and maintaining order during protests, sometimes using force to break up labor movements, which were seen as disruptive to the industrial order.

The Mid-20th Century: Civil Rights Era and Police Reforms (1950s - 1970s)

- **Civil Rights Movement**: The Civil Rights Movement in the 1950s and 1960s brought significant challenges to the traditional order in Durham. Like many other cities in the South, Durham was the site of protests, sit-ins, and other forms of civil disobedience as African Americans fought for desegregation and equal rights.

- **Police Response to Civil Rights Protests**: Durham police, like their counterparts across the South, were initially resistant to the demands for racial equality. In 1960, when African Americans began organizing sit-ins at segregated lunch counters in Durham, the police were often called to arrest protestors. The use of force and the mistreatment of activists became a focal point of criticism. Notably, police brutality during this time period contributed to a tense relationship between the police and African American communities in Durham.

"Black" Police Officers: As the Civil Rights Movement gained momentum, African Americans began advocating for greater representation within the police force. Beginning in the mid-1940s through the 1960s, some "Black" police officers began to serve within the Durham Police Department, although their roles were often limited, and they faced significant barriers within a department that was still deeply segregated in terms of power and authority.

The first 12 African American officers hired by the **Durham Police Department (DPD)** are an important part of the history of law enforcement and civil rights in Durham, North Carolina. Here are the names of some of the earliest African American officers who joined the DPD and were assigned to the Hayti District – a historically *"Black" Community*. These officers were pioneers, hired during a time of racial segregation and discrimination. Here are the names of some of the first African American officers in Durham, though this list might not represent the exact order in which they were hired:

First 12 African American Officers of the Durham Police Department: The Hayti Police

1. **James B. Samuel** – Hired in **1944**, James B. Samuel was the first African American (then referred to by whites as "Colored People") officer hired by the Durham Police Department. His hiring marked a significant shift toward racial integration in the department during the onset and turbulent period leading into the Civil Rights Movement.

2. **Clyde L. Cox** – Also hired in **1944**, Clyde L. Cox became one of the first "Black" officers to serve with the Durham Police Department, helping to bridge the divide between the "Black" community and law enforcement during a time of racial tension. Neither Cox nor Samuel were provided with uniforms. They could only arrest a Caucasian person if a white officer was present.

3. **Morris Williams** – Hired in the **1950s**, Williams was one of the early "Black" officers who helped build relations between the police and Durham's "Black" community despite facing significant racial challenges.

4. **James F. Williams** – Another early hire in the **1950s**, James F. Williams, worked alongside other early "Black" officers to help integrate the department and foster better relationships with "Black" Durham residents.

5. **Theodore "Ted" M. Thompson** – Hired in the **early 1960s**, Thompson was one of the first African American officers to rise in rank, eventually becoming a sergeant, and contributed to easing racial tensions between the police force and the community.

6. **Edward M. Green** – Hired in the **1960s**, Green was part of the growing number of African American officers who helped integrate the department during the Civil Rights Movement, serving as a trusted figure in the community.

7. **Charles E. Blackwell** – Hired in the **1960s**, Blackwell played a role in the early integration of the department, working alongside other African American officers to establish better rapport with the "Black" community.

8. **Alfred W. Green** – Also hired in the **1960s**, Alfred Green served during a time when the police department and the city were grappling with racial inequalities, and his role was vital in helping to bridge those gaps.

9. **Willie L. Brown** – Brown was one of the pioneering African American officers hired during the Civil Rights era, contributing to the gradual integration of the Durham Police Department.

10. **George W. McLaughlin** – McLaughlin served as one of the early "Black" officers, helping to reshape the relationship between law enforcement and Durham's African American neighborhoods.

11. **Samuel L. Sutton** – Sutton was another early "Black" officer who helped to pave the way for future African American officers in the Durham Police Department.

12. **O.C. Johnson** – A key early figure, O.C. Johnson was one of the African American officers who helped to create a more inclusive law enforcement system in Durham.

Honorable Mentions:

These individuals also played significant roles in the **Durham Police Department**, working as trailblazers in both investigative and patrol capacities:

1. **Lt. J.B. Samuel** – Lt. Samuel, who was previously mentioned. With his rising in rank he was an influential figure within the department and became one of the first "Black" officers to achieve a leadership role in Durham, serving as a *Lieutenant*. His contributions to law enforcement and racial integration were crucial in shaping the department.

2. **Detective Frank McCrea** – As one of the early *African American Detectives*, McCrea broke barriers within the department and

worked diligently in investigative roles, ensuring fair treatment in investigations involving "Black" citizens.

3. **Detective C.L. Cox** – Cox was not only one of the first "Black" officers but also a *Detective*, helping to integrate investigative functions within the department. His role was instrumental in demonstrating that African American officers could serve with distinction in all areas of law enforcement.

4. **Officer J.W. Price** – Price was an early African American officer who contributed to community policing efforts, establishing trust and bridging the divide between law enforcement and Durham's "Black" community.

5. **Officer C.W. Webb** – Webb, another important early officer, helped to support the integration of the police force, providing a valuable presence in the "Black" neighborhoods of Durham.

6. **Officer O.L. Harris** – Harris was an early "Black" officer who worked to increase the representation of African Americans within the department, playing a vital role in improving community relations.

7. **Officer W.N. Barnes** – Barnes served as a critical figure in the integration of the Durham Police Department, helping establish a foundation for future African American officers.

8. **Officer B.H. McClary** – McClary was an important African American officer who worked to ensure the representation and inclusion of "Black" citizens in law enforcement, serving as an example to future recruits.

9. **Officer O.W. Justice** – Justice worked to break down racial barriers within the department, becoming a respected officer who contributed to the department's evolution during a time of significant civil rights challenges.

10. **Officer Garson McLeod** – McLeod, like the other honorable mentions, played an integral role in helping to integrate the department and improve relations between the police and Durham's African American residents.

This list honors some of the pioneering African American officers and detectives who played an essential role in the integration of the Durham Police Department and served their community with distinction. These officers, starting with James B. Samuel and Clyde L. Cox, set the stage for future generations of African American law enforcement officers in Durham. Their work helped pave the way for a more inclusive and equitable police department despite the challenges they faced within the broader societal context of segregation and racial tension during the *Civil Rights Movement.* Their contributions were key in transforming the department and fostering better relations between law enforcement and the African American community in Durham.

While these names represent some of the early African American officers in Durham, it is important to note that the exact order and roles of these officers can likely be modified and expanded. These individuals, and others nonetheless, contributed to the evolving history of policing in Durham and helped pave the way for greater racial integration within the department.

When I was hired as a Durham Police Officer in 1986, there was one notable presence of the "legend" Detective, a remnant of those who paved the way for me, "Lo" Leathers. As for the names of those who could have been added to this list, I ask for your forgiveness for those pioneers not mentioned. In all fairness, every African American officer who preceded me can be likened to trailblazers, if not pioneers. Thank you for your service and sacrifice to the city we call home – ***Durham, The Bull City.***

Post-Civil Rights and Police Reform (1980s - 1990s)

- **Police and Racial Tensions**: While the 1970s and 1980s saw significant legal and social progress in the fight against racial segregation, tensions between the police and African American communities persisted. The police department's role in maintaining public order often translated into heavy-handed tactics in "Black" neighborhoods, especially in relation to issues like drug enforcement and youth crime.

- **The Rise of Community Policing**: During the late 20th century, there was a shift toward **community policing**, which sought to build stronger relationships between the police and the community, particularly in neighborhoods that had been marginalized or where tensions between the police and residents had historically been high. This approach sought to reduce crime by encouraging collaboration between the police and the communities they served. In Durham, this approach was part of a broader trend seen in many cities across the U.S.

Tony L. Scott

A Look at Hayti: Once Durham's
Thriving African American Hub

The Hayti District in Durham, North Carolina, holds a rich and significant history as a thriving African American community that became a focal point of "Black" life, culture, and activism during the early to mid-20th century. Its story is one of cultural resilience, community building, and eventual displacement due to *Gentrification and Urban Renewal policies.*

Hayti (pronounced "Hay-tee") was established in the late 19th century, during the post-Reconstruction era, and became known as a vibrant African American neighborhood. The district's name is often linked to the historical and symbolic significance of Haiti, which had a successful slave revolution and became the first independent "Black" republic in the world. The Hayti District – the first of its kind – a self-sustaining African American Community, grew as a center for "Black" economic, social, and cultural life, especially following *The Great Migration* when African Americans left the South for opportunities in cities across the North and South.

Spanning the early to mid-1900s, this vibrant community was not only a hub of "Black" life but also a thriving center for "Black" entertainment, with its boundaries marking a vital cultural and economic epicenter for African Americans in Durham and the broader region. The district's history intertwines with the rise of "Black-owned" businesses, civil rights activism, and a rich entertainment scene that made it a beacon for African American arts and culture.

Durham, in particular, emerged as an important hub for African American enterprise. By the early 20th century, Hayti was home to many

"Black-owned" businesses, including theaters, restaurants, and professional offices. The neighborhood also hosted educational institutions, churches, and social clubs, making it an important part of Durham's "Black" identity. One of the most notable landmarks in the area was the North Carolina Mutual Life Insurance Company, which was the largest "Black-owned" life insurance company in the U.S.

"Black" Police Officers in Hayti

The Hayti District was patrolled by a dedicated group of African American police officers who were part of the larger effort to protect and serve the "Black" community in an era when racial segregation and discrimination were deeply entrenched in the United States. African Americans in Durham, including the officers who served in Hayti, faced significant challenges given the racial dynamics of the time. While many white police officers were hostile to "Black" residents, the "Black" officers in Durham held an important role in bridging the gap between law enforcement and the "Black" community.

"Black" police officers in Durham were often seen as a stabilizing force within the Hayti District. They worked in an environment where racial tensions were high and where "Black" residents, despite being politically active and socially cohesive, were frequently subjected to unfair treatment by the predominantly white city authorities. The "Black" police officers in Durham not only patrolled the community but also served as role models and sources of empowerment. They were trusted by residents to handle local disputes and ensure the safety of the district in ways that aligned with the community's needs.

Their presence was critical in maintaining peace in a neighborhood that was an economic and cultural anchor for African Americans in Durham. These officers also played an important role in managing tensions during the Civil Rights Movement, acting as intermediaries between "Black" residents and white authorities, particularly during moments of social unrest.

Boundaries and Origins of Hayti District

Hayti's boundaries were roughly defined by what is now referred to as the western portion of downtown Durham. It included areas west of what is today the railroad tracks, near the intersection of Pettigrew Street and the surrounding neighborhoods. The core of the district extended from the east at the intersection of Fayetteville and Main Streets, curving westward to include parts of the more residential areas south of the railroad.

Hayti was situated between the "Black" and white sections of Durham, but it quickly became a dominant "Black" business and residential community. Over time, the district flourished! The area was originally established after the Civil War as African Americans began settling in Durham, many of whom had been freed from slavery and were seeking economic opportunities. The district emerged during a period when "Black" Durhamites were pushing for autonomy, self-sufficiency, and better living conditions. The district expanded with the growth of institutions like North Carolina Mutual Life Insurance Company and the Mechanics and Farmers Bank, which were among the first major "Black-owned" corporations in the U.S.

Hayti, like other historically "Black" communities, was developed as a space where African Americans could build and control their own businesses, educational institutions, and cultural institutions without interference from white communities.

Hayti as a Mecca for Black Entertainment

One of Hayti's most distinctive features during its peak years was its vibrant and diverse entertainment scene. The district was considered a mecca for "Black" entertainment, not just in Durham, but in the southeastern United States. Given the segregated nature of society at the time, "Black" communities across the South created their own cultural spaces to express themselves artistically, and Hayti was at the forefront of this cultural movement.

Key Venues and Performers

The Hayti District was home to numerous theaters, clubs, and venues that attracted some of the most prominent "Black" entertainers of the era. Notable venues included the *Duke Theatre* (which was built by the Duke family and became one of the most important spaces for "Black" artists) and the *Royal Cabaret*, a popular spot for jazz, blues, and gospel performances. These venues hosted some of the most famous musicians, including legendary figures like *James Brown, Duke Ellington, Billie Holiday, Ella Fitzgerald, Louis Armstrong, and Count Basie.* The area was a key stop on the so-called "Chitlin' Circuit," a network of venues across the South where "Black" entertainers performed due to segregation policies that barred them from performing in white establishments.

The Baby Grand was also a notable nightclub located at 915 Ramseur Street in Durham's historic Hayti District. During its heyday, particularly in the 1970s, it was a vibrant venue for local soul and disco performers.

The Baby Grand, alongside other venues like the Stallion Club, played a significant role in Durham's rich music scene, offering a space for both local and touring acts to perform and for the community to gather and celebrate their cultural heritage.

The club's popularity was part of a larger ecosystem of "Soul Spots" that supported the burgeoning R&B and soul music culture in Durham. Its role in fostering the city's musical and social fabric underscores the historical significance of Hayti as a center of African American resilience and creativity. Interestingly, I recall one of my family members making a specific mention of the Baby Grand and how Durham Hayti was a grand theater before its take over by the white power structure and what downtown Durham has become.

This era saw Hayti become a hotbed for jazz and blues music, with local clubs offering nightly performances by regional talent while national stars toured through Durham, cementing the district's reputation as an entertainment hub. Churches in the area also became key cultural centers, often hosting gospel performances and bringing communities together through music and worship.

Cultural Institutions

In addition to live performances, Hayti also became home to other cultural and social organizations. The *Hayti Heritage Center,* once a church, is one of the few remaining symbols of the district's entertainment and cultural past. It was a gathering space for both arts performances and political discussions, becoming an important community institution that helped nurture "Black" artists and activists.

Furthermore, the district also hosted *The North Carolina Mutual Life Insurance Company and Mechanics & Farmers Bank*, which supported the "Black" middle and upper class, who could afford to attend the area's growing cultural events and patronize local businesses. The presence of such institutions gave Hayti an economic base that enabled its thriving entertainment and arts scene to flourish!

The Impact of Gentrification and the Decline of Hayti

Despite its success and cultural significance, the Hayti District began to face significant challenges after the mid-20th century, primarily due to *Gentrification and Urban Renewal* efforts. As the city of Durham sought to modernize and revitalize downtown, Hayti became a target for demolition and redevelopment.

The 1950s and 1960s saw the federal government's urban renewal programs implemented in Durham, which disproportionately impacted "Black" communities, particularly the Hayti District. In the name of "progress" and "revitalization," much of Hayti was bulldozed to make way for new commercial developments, highways, and public housing. The construction of the Durham Freeway (I-147) in the 1970s led to the destruction of a significant portion of the district. The very core of Hayti's cultural and commercial life was decimated, and thousands of residents and business owners were displaced.

The loss of these businesses and entertainment venues contributed to the economic and social decline of the area. Gentrification in the latter part of the 20th century further displaced long-time residents, and today, while some parts of the Hayti District remain, much of its original character – especially its entertainment and "Black" cultural institutions – has been lost. The district's history is now largely remembered through cultural preservation efforts, local historical markers, and institutions like the Hayti Heritage Center, which work to educate the public about the district's rich legacy.

As a child growing up in the Fayetteville Street Housing Development, I remember walking to the store and getting my hair cut a *Thorpe's Barber Shop*. This miniature business area was located behind what is now *The Hayti Heritage Center* and adjacent to what was Fayetteville Street Housing Development. Other small business shops were located on this small plot of land. These businesses were housed together but separate in a continues structure made of cheap metal and tin. Hence, the location became known as "Tin City." This is where the displaced business owners who once thrived before *Gentrification and Urban Renewal* had to relocate to when their land, in a sense was stolen. For a short time before the area was redeveloped, I patrolled this location as a rookie police officer.

Legacy of Hayti

Despite the physical destruction of the district, the legacy of Hayti as a cultural and entertainment hub remains alive in Durham's African American community. The history of Hayti continues to be celebrated in local history museums, cultural festivals, and by the descendants of those who lived and thrived there. The contributions of Hayti's "Black" police officers, who helped maintain order during times of racial and civil unrest, are also remembered as part of the district's complex and empowering story.

Hayti's cultural significance as a center for "Black" entertainment reminds us of the resilience of African American communities in the face of systemic racism and economic hardship. While the district's physical landscape may have changed, the cultural impact of its music, businesses, and activism endures.

James E. Shepard was one of the founding fathers of Hayti, along with Aaron McDuffie Moore, John Merrick and Charles Clinton Spaulding. Shepard, Moore and Merrick founded the North Carolina Mutual Life Insurance Company (1898), which became the largest and richest African American company in the United States at the time. It had a land development company as a subsidiary, which helped build much of Hayti. The prosperous African American funeral homeowner J. C. Scarborourgh and his wife Daisy built the Scarborough House at 1406 Fayetteville St.

Early 21st Century: Modern Issues and Reforms (2000s - Present)

- **Police-Community Relations**: The 21st century saw continued focus on improving police-community relations, particularly with Durham's "Black" community. Issues like racial profiling, police brutality, and the disproportionate targeting of African Americans for drug-related offenses remained a significant concern. In response to public pressure, there were increasing calls for transparency and accountability within the Durham Police Department.

- **High-Profile Incidents**: Durham's police department faced criticism following high-profile incidents such as the Duke University lacrosse case in 2006. The case involved accusations of sexual assault made by an African American woman against members of the predominantly white lacrosse team. The subsequent handling of the case by Durham police and the district attorney sparked controversy over race, class, and law enforcement practices.

- **Police Reforms**: In response to national calls for reform, especially after events like the *2014 Ferguson unrest* and the *Black Lives Matter movement*, Durham has taken steps toward addressing racial bias and enhancing accountability in policing. These reforms included better training for officers in community engagement, de-escalation tactics, and the introduction of body cameras to increase transparency. However, challenges remain in fully rebuilding trust between the police department and the City's African American community.

- **Diversification and Inclusion**: The Durham Police Department has made efforts to diversify its force, aiming to better reflect the racial and cultural makeup of the city. It has also increased its focus on issues like mental health crises and domestic violence through specialized training and response units.

- **Continued Tensions and Calls for Reform**: Like many other police departments across the country, Durham's police force has faced scrutiny over its handling of issues like excessive use of force and racial disparities in arrests, especially in relation to "Black" and Latino communities. The aftermath of incidents like the **2016 shooting death of Keith Lamont Scott** in nearby Charlotte and protests for racial justice have contributed to ongoing calls for police reform, including demands for changes in training, policies on the use of force, and oversight mechanisms.

The history of policing in Durham, North Carolina, reflects broader trends in American law enforcement. From its early days as a force tasked with enforcing Jim Crow laws and maintaining racial segregation to its role in suppressing civil rights activism, the Durham Police Department has been intertwined with issues of race, power, and social justice. While there have been periods of reform, the department continues to grapple with its historical legacy and the challenges of building trust and equity in a city that remains racially diverse and politically active. The future of policing in Durham, like elsewhere, depends on ongoing efforts to ensure transparency, accountability, and a commitment to racial justice.

Since I retired as a police officer, I've given thought to retired Police Officers being invited to the table to share their wisdom and knowledge. I believe the Durham Community can greatly benefit from such collaboration.

Policing In North America

The evolution of police departments in North America has been deeply influenced by various societal changes, including the rise of urbanization, the development of modern law enforcement, and the enforcement of racial control, particularly through institutions like *Slave Patrols*. The history of policing is intertwined with the growth of racial inequality, and the legacy of police involvement in slavery and racial oppression continues to affect policing practices today.

1. Early Policing and the Development of Slave Patrols (1600s - 1700s)

Colonial Policing

- **Informal Systems**: In the early days of colonial America, policing was informal and based largely on community self-regulation. In northern colonies, rudimentary systems like night watches and constables were established to monitor crime and maintain order. However, in the southern colonies, where plantation economies relied heavily on enslaved labor, policing took on a much darker role.

- **Slave Patrols**: One of the most significant forms of early police forces in the American South was the **slave patrol**. These patrols were organized by local governments and were composed of white men who were tasked with controlling and surveilling the enslaved African population. Slave patrols had several core functions:

  - **Surveillance and Control**: They monitored the movements of enslaved people, ensuring they did not gather in large numbers and preventing uprisings or escape attempts.

  - **Punishment and Intimidation**: Patrols were empowered to punish enslaved individuals who were found disobeying orders or attempting to escape, often through brutal means.

  - **Preventing Rebellions**: The patrols sought to suppress any potential revolts and were involved in tracking down runaway slaves. They were known to patrol areas outside plantations and even into towns or cities.

o **Legal Authority**: These patrols had the legal backing to arrest, beat, and sometimes kill those who were considered threats to the system of slavery. They were one of the earliest forms of formalized law enforcement in the southern colonies and were specifically designed to protect the institution of slavery.

- **Legacy of Slave Patrols**: Slave patrols directly influenced the development of policing in the southern United States. Many of the duties associated with maintaining order in these patrols evolved into the functions of future law enforcement agencies. As a result, many of the racial control aspects of modern police forces in the U.S. can be traced back to the system of slave patrols.

2. Formation of Modern Police Forces (1800s)

- **Growth of Urban Policing**: By the early 19th century, as American cities grew due to industrialization, the informal and often ineffective community-based systems of policing gave way to more formalized city police forces. In 1838, Boston established the first paid, professional police force in the U.S., followed by the New York Police Department (NYPD) in 1845. These forces were primarily tasked with maintaining public order, responding to crime, and managing the social issues of the day, such as poverty, immigration, and labor unrest.

- **Racial Overtones in Policing**: While slave patrols had been largely focused on the control of enslaved people, the early police forces in urban centers also targeted immigrant groups, the poor, and racial minorities. Policing in these cities often involved efforts to suppress working-class movements and protect the interests of the wealthy elite.

- **Expansion of Police Roles**: As the role of police forces grew, especially with the rise of organized crime and the political machine system, many early U.S. police departments were still marked by corruption and close ties to local political entities. The focus on maintaining order through sometimes violent means laid the groundwork for the militarized police tactics that would later emerge.

3. Late 19th and Early 20th Century: Police and Racial Control

- **Reconstruction and the Rise of Racialized Policing**: Following the Civil War and the abolition of slavery, the South saw the rise of laws like the *Black Codes*, which severely restricted the rights of freed "Black" people. Police forces, including those in the South, played a role in enforcing racial segregation, curfews, and labor restrictions on "Black" people.

  o **The Role of Police in Jim Crow**: Under the system of Jim Crow, which legalized racial segregation in the South from the late 19th century to the mid-20th century, police forces were tasked with upholding segregation and maintaining control over "Black" populations. Police in the South often violently suppressed Black civil rights activists and those who challenged the system.

- **Police Brutality and Civil Rights Struggles**: By the early to mid-20th century, especially during the Civil Rights Movement, police forces gained national attention for their brutality in suppressing peaceful protests. Famous incidents, such as the violent response to the *March on Washington* and the *Selma to Montgomery marches*, highlighted the deep-rooted racism within law enforcement. These actions can be seen as an extension of the legacy of slave patrols, as the police continued to function as agents of racial control.

4. Mid-20th Century to Present: Militarization and Continued Racial Tensions

- **Post-WWII and War on Drugs**: After World War II, the role of police departments expanded, and new tactics were developed to address growing crime in cities. The *War on Drugs in the 1980s* further escalated the militarization of police forces, particularly in urban areas with high minority populations. In these contexts, the legacy of controlling marginalized groups through the police was clear.

  o **Militarization**: Police forces began adopting military-style equipment and tactics, including S.W.A.T. Teams, armored vehicles, and increased surveillance. The emphasis on controlling crime, particularly drug-related crimes, disproportionately affected African American and Latino communities. These tactics, while ostensibly designed to address crime, often led to increased instances of police brutality and the mass incarceration of people of color.

- **Reform Movements and Continued Struggles**: The Civil Rights Movement of the 1960s and subsequent movements like *Black Lives Matter* have drawn attention to the persistent racial bias within police forces. Activists argue that the modern police force, despite reforms, still carries the legacy of its origins in slave patrols, with its focus on controlling and surveilling marginalized communities.

- **Calls for Police Reform and Abolition**: The rise of movements like *Defund the Police* and calls for abolition stem from the understanding that police in North America were historically created to protect the interests of the powerful (such as slaveowners and wealthy elites) and continue to disproportionately target marginalized communities. Reform proposals have focused on reducing the militarization of police, increasing community-based alternatives to policing, and addressing systemic racism within law enforcement.

5. The Legacy of Slave Patrols in Modern Policing

- **Racial Disparities**: The most enduring impact of the slave patrol system on modern policing is the continuing pattern of racialized policing. African Americans, particularly men, are disproportionately targeted, subjected to violence, and incarcerated. The historical role of police in enforcing slavery, segregation, and racial inequality remains a critical factor in understanding contemporary issues like police brutality and racial profiling.

- **Ongoing Struggles for Justice**: Activists and scholars argue that the roots of policing in slave patrols continue to influence the practices and culture of modern police departments. The demand for police reform, accountability, and abolition is seen as an effort to sever this historical connection and address the systemic racism ingrained in law enforcement.

The evolution of police departments in North America cannot be separated from the history of racial oppression, particularly through institutions like slave patrols. These patrols laid the foundation for modern police forces in the southern United States and influenced how policing functions to this day, with a legacy of controlling marginalized communities and maintaining racial hierarchies. As society continues to grapple with police reform and accountability, it remains essential to recognize the historical origins of policing in racialized control and the continuing impact on communities of color.

As I close, I want to emphasize that the public's perception of their local *Policing Agencies* cannot be underestimated! I believe there are two things that a Police Department can implement easily so that the community they serve may have trust in them and maintain a lasting partnership: Total transparency when addressing questionable practices of their officers. And their findings are shared without delay!

CHAPTER 2

A New Beginning, A Hard Road: From Soldier to Sentinel

It was the late winter of 1983. I signed a commitment letter to join the United States Army. After completing high school in June of 1983, I was transported to the Raleigh Army Duty Station, where I swore an oath to serve my country. There shortly afterward, I was flown off to El Paso, Texas, to begin basic training at Fort Bliss.

While going through basic training with "A Battery 2nd Platoon 3rd BN 1st ADA TNG BDG," I experienced racism in a way I had never encountered before. For some reason, a white Drill Instructor, Staff Sergeant Grimm, singled me out. He said something and questioned me along these lines with a measure of a challenging judgment of me, "You must be from up North – Chicago or Detroit?" My self-confidence, I guess, he took exception to. These brothers, who were from up North, had an air, a swag, a street and self-awareness about themselves... they were not pushovers or easily intimidated by anyone, let alone someone white. Despite the challenges, I was performing well and had been promoted to squad leader, overseeing at least a dozen men.

Later, I was entrusted with overseeing the entire platoon. Unbeknownst to me, a well-respected and strong drill sergeant, Staff Sergeant Dorsey – an African American man – was serving as a buffer for me. Unfortunately, during this period, his mother passed away, and he had to leave temporarily. While he was away, my white comrades, the very men I was training to serve alongside, lied and conspired against me to undermine my credibility and leadership role for their own gain. It was no problem for them to get in the ear of Drill Sergeant Grimm, who had questioned me and Staff Sergeant Danyaun, his counterpart.

After wrongly accusing me and usurping my leadership to gain power, these disreputable soldiers chose to abuse their authority by smoking in the barracks. One evening, they left the facility unauthorized to party and do whatever else they chose to do. Upon Staff Sergeant Dorsey's return, he asked me what had happened. I informed him of their actions, but there was nothing he could do at that point. Nevertheless, justice prevailed! These individuals who had undermined my authority and conspired against me because of their own wrongdoing were either discharged from the military or recycled. Just the same, I never saw them (McClusky, Gentry and Sloan) again.

I felt vindicated once these individuals were dismissed from the Army or recycled. Nevertheless, I was not reinstated to the position of platoon guide that I once held. However, I successfully completed basic training, after which I began training for my Military Occupational Service (MOS). After about two months, this training had also been completed. I would continue on with training at Fort Benning, Georgia, so that I may become an 82nd Airborne Paratrooper at Fort Bragg.

I was well-prepared for the physical demands of training, as well as the mental capacity needed to endure both basic training and *Jump School*. However, what I was not prepared for was the racism I encountered – not only during basic training but also upon arriving at Fort Bragg. These experiences tested me in ways I had never imagined!

Thanks to my mother and her encouragement during basic training and encouraging me to *"Find Jesus for myself,"* a faith that I had not known began to develop. That faith and God's *Favor* or *Grace* ultimately sustained me – not only through my time in the military but also through the years I would dedicate to serving my community in Durham, also known as The Bull City.

Arriving at Fort Bragg, located in Fayetteville, North Carolina – marked another significant chapter in my journey. (Recently, in 2023, Fort Bragg, named after a Confederate leader, was renamed Fort Liberty.) My duty assignment was Charlie Battery, 3/ 4th Air Defense Artillery Regiment (ADA). Upon joining the unit, I discovered that the squad I was assigned to had been nicknamed the "Brody Plantation" before my arrival. I would soon learn why.

Our Staff Sergeant, Staff Sergeant Tindall, operated as if he were a dictator. His demeanor was unlike anything I had encountered. Even the leaders under his command were visibly intimidated by him, often cowering in his presence. This was something I could not, and would not, tolerate... to be intimidated by another person!

While stationed at Fort Bragg, I also encountered both subtle and overt racism, which added to the challenges I faced. However, what struck me as equally puzzling was the pervasive fear among the men I served with under Staff Sergeant Tindall. Such was their fear of him that they had developed a code phrase: *Red Tite!* Whenever someone spotted Staff Sergeant Tindall approaching, the phrase *Red Tite!* was called out, and grown men would immediately jump to action, busying themselves to avoid his wrath and threats.

From these experiences, I reached my breaking point. Enough was enough!

There came a tipping point during my time at Fort Bragg – a situation that caused me to decide to go AWOL. At that moment, it was my intention never to return to the military. However, my mother, with her wisdom and guidance, convinced me otherwise. Upon my return, I informed my chain of command about the reason for my absence. I sat before my commander and expressed my concerns, making it clear that I wanted to leave the military. His response was, "First, I will have you attend (either it was a 30-day or a 60-day) training for rehabilitation / correctional purposes at the Central Custody Facility (CCF)."

Day 1, CCF: Stripped for Duty

Although I had agreed to attend the CCF facility, my desire to leave the military remained unchanged. Standing in the orderly room of the CCF, a large open space, I was processed in while my platoon sergeant stood nearby, having escorted me there. I was assigned the roster # 225. From that point on, I was no longer addressed by my name and rank but only as *roster # 225*. If I wished to speak with any of the commanding officers, I had to say, "Roster # 225, request permission to speak."

While standing there, I needed to use the restroom, or as it was called, the latrine. I respectfully asked several times, saying, "Roster # 225, request permission to speak." Each time, my request was denied to utilize the latrine. Once again, enough was enough! I left my position of "At-ease" and marched directly to the latrine! As I did, I was closely and hurriedly followed by a member of the CCF commanding team and the sergeant (both white males) who had escorted me to the facility.

Having completed my business, I was met with glaring stares and an intimidating look from the commanding officers. The CCF commanding officer immediately questioned me about what I was doing. I replied, "I needed to use the latrine, and you didn't allow me to. So, I took it upon myself to go. My attitude was – Now what?!"

What followed was a surprise, though I now understand it was part of the process to check for contraband. I was ordered to remove every article of clothing, every thread. Afterward, I was told to do 10 or 20 push-ups. Once commanded, I was told to perform an about-face and do another 10 to 20 push-ups.

It was the heat of the Summer, and I began to sweat profusely. But more than the physical strain, I was agitated – frustrated to the point where I started taunting them. I made comments like, "You wish your body was like mine... you envy me... don't you?!" At that moment, it was clear: I was intent on getting kicked out of the military. Although my language and tone were disrespectful, I still obeyed the commands to perform the push-ups.

What I now realize is that there seemed to be a limit to how many push-ups could be done in one stretch. That's why I was ordered to do an about-face and then immediately perform more. As a result of my actions, I was threatened with another disciplinary measure. I was told I would have to go through the "Old Course" – an obstacle course with about a dozen obstacles that I would have to run through, navigating over and under various barriers within a set time.

Given my physical conditioning, this course was not a challenge for me at all. However, after numerous push-ups and intense physical activity, I woke up the next day experiencing extreme soreness and tightness in my upper extremities. Medically, I later learned this was likely Delayed Onset Muscle Soreness (DOMS), though the pain and stiffness I felt was far more extreme than anything I had ever experienced before!

My initial defiance after reporting to CCF didn't get me dismissed from the military, so I settled in and continued to be the good Soldier I had always been. I did what was required of me and was well on my way to being released early. There was some kind of grading system they had in place based on one's conduct, and one of the staff members informed me that if I continued on this track, I would be released early.

However, a young white sergeant, perhaps around 25 years old, was assigned to CCF. He was in as good of physical condition as I was. For whatever reason, likely racism – nothing new – he sought to intimidate me. But this would not work against me! There were times when he would attempt to stare me down, unwavering I would simply stare back at him, unflinching!

However, things would soon escalate! There was a moment when I was about to exit the barracks, just as this young sergeant was entering. Neither of us made any attempt to yield. As we passed, our shoulders bumped. He looked at me, and I looked back at him, but I continued on my way without saying a word.

From that point on, he had it out for me! Shortly thereafter, another CCF staff member (a w/m), someone who knew I had been performing well, asked me what was going on. I told him that this new sergeant had it in for me. He simply looked at me, not saying anything in response. But it was clear from his expression that he understood exactly what was happening.

Unfortunately, I was not released early from CCF. Despite that, I continued to perform my duties well, keeping my focus on doing my job. Eventually, I was returned to my duty station. Upon returning, I made it clear to my command staff once again that I wanted to be released from the military. I expressed my desire to leave, just as I had before.

Deception

But what followed was a deception I had not expected! My commander knew that I was a good soldier; additionally, the Government had spent quite a bit of money on my training. My commanding officer, therefore, led me to believe that I would soon receive my discharge papers. Some days or weeks later, instead of receiving my discharge, I was handed orders. Orders to deploy to Wachernheim, Germany. I was devastated! This was not the outcome I had hoped for, and the disappointment weighed heavy on me! Nevertheless, for reasons that I can't explain, I reported to my next duty station. Well, let me say otherwise; God, in His infinite wisdom and favor, established my course without me realizing the matter.

After honorably serving approximately two and a half years in the military, the Government, in an effort to cut spending, began offering early discharges to soldiers who had less than six months remaining in their service. Without hesitation, I seized this opportunity!

I returned to the United States with my military assignment successfully completed. I received an *Honorable Discharge, with the rank – Specialist E-4,* including a few awards and metals. I now know that by the grace of God and the prayers of my mother, I was not allowed to have my way or get out of the military on my terms. If things had gone as I desired, this tale and my life's story would have been disastrously different! Just days before I arrived back home to the "States," in March of 1986, I had turned 21 years old.

As I considered my next steps professionally, I began to look into becoming a police officer... the age requirement was 21 years of age. This line of work was paramilitary; therefore, I thought this would be a great fit. Unfortunately, I didn't have a skill set that would have provided me a meaningful career outside of policing. I applied to both the Chapel Hill Police Department and the Duke University Police Department, both located in North Carolina. To my delight, both departments offered me a job.

However, I declined the Chapel Hill offer because their role in public safety included not just policing but also fighting fires, which didn't align with what I envisioned for my future. My thinking regarding fighting fires; with all the gear firefighters had to wear, weather-wise, there was not an ideal condition to do this job. While serving in the military, I had to work, eat and sleep under the night skies, no matter the weather conditions. Therefore, I gave firefighting a pass. I also declined the job offer from Duke University Police Department. Ultimately, I accepted the job with the Durham Police Department in the city where I was born and raised. I was thrilled that I had been offered the Job!

Returning Home and the Path to Law Enforcement

After my time in the military, as mentioned, I returned home in March of 1986 with a clear sense of purpose: I wanted to become a police officer! The values and discipline instilled in me during my military service had solidified my commitment to serve and protect my community. I quickly began the process of filling out applications to local law enforcement agencies, setting my sights on joining the ranks of those who are sworn to *Protect and Serve* the community.

While I awaited responses, I kept myself busy by working two different jobs over the Summer and into the Fall, making use of the work ethic I had developed in the military. It was a long and uncertain period, but I remained determined. The hiring process to become a police officer was as rigorous as it should have been, involving multiple stages to ensure the suitability and preparedness of candidates for such a demanding role.

The Rigorous Vetting Process

The application process was thorough, and rightly so. Candidates were required to meet a host of standards, with each step serving as a critical assessment of their readiness and ability to perform the duties of a police officer. Among the tests I faced were the following:

- **Psychological Evaluation**: This assessment ensured candidates possessed the mental fortitude and stability needed to handle the pressures of the job.

- **Drug Testing**: A necessary step to confirm fitness for duty and adherence to professional standards.

- **Background Check**: This extensive process involved examining my past conduct, personal history, and character. It was vital to demonstrate that I could uphold the law with integrity.

- **Physical Fitness Test**: As the job required peak physical conditioning, this assessment measured strength, endurance, and overall readiness.

- **Written Exam**: This test evaluated communication skills and problem-solving abilities, both essential for effective law enforcement.

Oral Review Board / Interview Process:

During the Oral Review Board, I sat before a panel of 3 to 5 commanding police officers who asked me various questions. This part of the process was designed to assess my truthfulness and suitability for the role. Questions ranged from whether I had ever used drugs or taken medication that was not prescribed to me to why I wanted to become a police officer, along with other probing inquiries. I fared well, navigating the questions with honesty and confidence.

This vetting process stretched across the summer months, adding to the anticipation and uncertainty. It was both a test of patience and a testament to the commitment required to serve.

Becoming a Sentinel of Durham as a Police Officer

Finally, the waiting came to an end. To my great delight, I received calls from several of the agencies I had applied to. The sense of accomplishment was profound, but the decision was clear: I would choose to serve my community. This choice marked the beginning of a new chapter in my life, one rooted in service to my hometown and community – *The Bull City!*

On November 10, 1986, I officially began my journey with Police Academy No. 2. Prior to Academy No. 1., a year earlier, the Durham Police Department was Durham Public Safety like Chapel Hill. The City of Durham recognized that as it grew in size and population, dividing law enforcement from firefighting would best serve the Durham community.

Excited about my future, the academy was the next step in transforming me from a military-trained soldier into a sentinel of The Bull City. It was here that I would learn the skills and knowledge specific to law enforcement, building on the foundation of discipline and resilience instilled in me by the military.

Police Academy No. 2, which I would be in, held its training at the Fire Department's training facility located at 2008 E. Club Blvd. During this time, the Police Department Headquarters was located at 302 North Mangum Street and Holloway Street (1960s–1991). The department was located in a Government building complex shared with City Hall. This facility served as police headquarters for several decades before the move to 505 West Chapel Hill Street (1991–2018); from said location, I retired as a Durham Police Officer. This was a relocation to the former Home Security Life Building, a location that served as the DPD headquarters for over 30 years before moving to a purpose-built facility. In 2018, the department moved to a modern, specially constructed headquarters at 602 East Main Street. This location was designed to meet the growing needs of the police department and improve its efficiency.

Police Academy: Day One

Day one of the police academy is a blur, as is much of my 27 years of service as a police officer in the Bull City. It was an overwhelming mix of emotions – anticipation, pride, and uncertainty! Walking into Police Academy No. 2, I was aware that this was the beginning of a transformative journey. Yet, the intensity of the moment, coupled with the sheer volume of information, left much of that day a hazy memory.

At this stage of training, we were not handed a badge and certainly not a firearm! These tools and symbols had to be earned through hard work, both mentally and physically! However, we were each issued a uniform to wear, symbolizing our commitment to the process and the expectations placed upon us. The uniform was a constant reminder that the academy was not merely about completing tasks but about embodying the discipline, unity, integrity, and professionalism required of law enforcement officers.

What I do remember vividly is the sense of camaraderie forming among us recruits, the stern but guiding presence of the instructors, and the first glimpse of what it truly meant to dedicate oneself to public service. It was clear from the start that becoming a police officer was not merely a job – it was a calling demanding the utmost discipline, focus, and commitment!

Leadership and Change at the Durham Police Department

When I joined the Durham Police Department as a new recruit, the Chief of Police was Chief T. Lassiter. His leadership represented a continuation of traditional practices within the department. However, significant change came with the appointment of Trevor Hampton as the first African American Chief of Police. This was a monumental move that signaled a shift away from the old ways of doing things, challenging the entrenched "good old boy" mentality that had long influenced the department.

Chief Hampton's tenure was groundbreaking, but it was not without its challenges. He faced significant opposition, not only because of the color of his skin but also due to some of the decisions he made as chief. If memory serves correctly, those choices, as well as his personal life, made him a target for critics who were resistant to change and uncomfortable with the idea of an African American at the helm of the police department. Despite this opposition, Chief Hampton's leadership was pivotal in fostering a new direction and mentality within the Durham Police Department – one of progress and inclusivity. His contributions were substantial, even if they have not always been recognized or celebrated to the extent they deserve.

Following Chief Hampton, the department saw another historic milestone with the appointment of its first female Chief of Police, Teresa Chambers. Her leadership style brought a fresh perspective to the department. She was succeeded by Chief Jackie McNeil, followed by Chief Steve Chalmers, each of whom left their mark on the organization in unique ways.

When I retired, the department was under the leadership of Chief Jose Lopez. Each of these leaders shaped the culture and direction of the Durham Police Department during my 27 years of service, navigating challenges while continuing to move the department forward.

Police Academy Training

As I share my law enforcement experience with the Durham Police Department over 27 years, I will do my best to share information that may interest you. The stories and details I recount will come solely from my memory, as I did not keep a diary of my nearly three decades in law enforcement. This is something I've often encouraged new officers to do. Documenting their experiences can serve as a meaningful way to reflect on how they've served the Durham community and leave behind a legacy for their loved ones.

Once the police academy training began, life took on a rigid structure for the next five months. Regardless of the weather – be it rain, sleet, or snow – we had to report for class promptly every morning at about six o'clock. The day always began with physical training (PT), which tested our stamina and discipline. Each morning started with calisthenics and warm-up exercises to prepare our bodies, followed by running a specific number of miles or completing a set distance to build endurance and mental toughness. A few of the cadets really struggled with their physical conditioning. On our days off, I chose to meet with these classmates to help them improve their physical and mental conditioning. L.B. and R.D. are the initials of two of my classmates that I readily recall helping. There may have been others; I'm quite sure there were.

After PT, the rest of the day was dedicated to the learning process. The training was intense, covering a range of state-mandated courses designed to prepare us for the diverse challenges of law enforcement. These courses included:

- **Report Writing**: Learning how to clearly and accurately document incidents, a skill crucial to ensuring justice and accountability.

46

- **Accident Investigation**: Mastering the analysis of crash scenes and the preparation of "10 50" reports, commonly known as accident reports.

- **Criminal and Civil Law**: Developing a deep understanding of the laws we were sworn to uphold, ensuring we could enforce them fairly and effectively.

- **City Ordinances**: Familiarizing ourselves with the ordinances specific to Durham, North Carolina, so we could properly enforce local regulations.

- **Motor Vehicle Law**: Studying the laws governing the operation of vehicles within North Carolina, a critical aspect of maintaining public safety on the roads.

- **Driver's Training**: Also known as defensive driving, this course included techniques for high-stress driving scenarios and conducting felony stops.

- **First Aid and CPR**: Learning lifesaving skills to respond to medical emergencies in the field.

The training also included critical tactical skills:

- **Firearms Training**: At the range, we learned to handle and shoot our standard-issue .38 caliber handguns and 12-gauge shotguns with precision and care.

- **Self-Defense**: Training sessions taught us how to protect ourselves and others in physical confrontations. Additionally, how to effectively utilize our nightsticks and proper handcuffing techniques.

- **Chemical Identification**: We were trained to use manuals to identify hazardous chemicals transported along highways, ensuring public safety in potentially dangerous situations.

Finally, we learned the essentials of effective communication, including:

- **Police Radio Etiquette**: Mastering the use of 10 codes and maintaining professionalism on the airwaves.

These lessons were complemented by hands-on experiences, such as defensive driving and felony stop scenarios, which tested our ability to react under pressure. The combination of physical, academic, and tactical training made it clear that the academy was designed to transform us from civilians into capable, disciplined law enforcement officers. This list of training is rather thorough. However, it is not complete with all that was taught in the academy.

The Grading Process and Class Recognition

Throughout the five months of training, there was a rigorous grading process. While I don't remember the exact requirements, certain classes and disciplines demanded minimum scores to pass. Each task was a measure of readiness and competency. Even physical training was graded, requiring cadets to meet time goals for running a mile and minimum standards for push-ups and sit-ups.

As the academy concluded, awards were handed out to recognize outstanding cadets. Three of these awards stand out in my memory. The first was awarded to the most studious cadet – recognizing the individual whose grades ranked highest in the class. The second was for the most physically fit cadet; lastly Firearms Marksmanship. I am proud to say that I received the award for being most physically fit – the *Physical Training Award*. It was based on performance across multiple physical challenges, including running the fastest mile, completing the greatest number of push-ups, and excelling in overall strength exercises such as the bench press. The combined scores across three or four exercises earned me the trophy for physical fitness, a recognition that meant a great deal to me!

Graduation Day

Police Academy No. 2, the class I proudly belonged to, may have started out with as many as 22 cadets when training began. By the time graduation arrived on April 3, 1987, we may have lost two or three cadets along the way for various reasons. Despite these losses, graduation day was a time of immense thrill and high delight!

During the five months of training in the academy, we absorbed a wealth of information – some of it retained, some inevitably forgotten over the years. Yet, even now, nearly four decades later, I vividly remember three key pieces of advice shared by one of my training officers.

The first was, **"One bad officer can cause a negative reflection on the entire Durham Police Department."** Those words stuck with me because they underscored the immense responsibility that came with wearing the badge. Our individual actions, whether honorable or dishonorable, could shape the reputation of an entire department.

The second piece of advice was about personal pride: **"The way you wear your uniform – with pride or without – is a reflection of how you carry yourself and how you want others to perceive you."** Over the course of my law enforcement career, I found this to be profoundly true. The way we presented ourselves influenced not only public perception but also the pride and professionalism we brought to the job.

The third piece of advice was a practical one but equally significant: **"You all, as police officers, have training unlike the general population. Be sure to carry your weapons with you when you are off duty. You never know if you may have to intervene as a police officer to protect the community, your family, and not the least of which yourself."** This advice reflected the reality that law enforcement is not a job one step away from when the shift ends.

The duty to serve and protect extends beyond the uniform, and that sense of vigilance became a part of me throughout my career. Even now, it is a mentality that has not dissipated. I call it a double-edged sword; in these days and times it serves as a benefit to be aware of your surroundings. However, with this comes a measure of stress that I have found is always upon me.

Graduation day itself was a proud culmination of this intense training. Family members and friends gathered to celebrate our accomplishments. Dressed sharply in our duty uniforms, we received our badges – a symbol of the responsibility and honor we were about to carry. The excitement was palpable as we prepared to step into the next chapter of our lives!

Graduation was not the end of our training but the beginning of hands-on experience. After the ceremony, we were assigned to our respective duty stations, where, in a matter of days, we began the *Field Training Officer*

(FTO) Program. This phase was crucial for bridging the gap between the academy and the realities of police work, pairing us with experienced officers to guide and mentor us through the practical application of everything we had learned.

However, not everyone who started in Police Academy No. 2 remained with the department until retirement. For various reasons, including death, some of my academy classmates left law enforcement before completing their careers. Their absence over the years serves as a reminder of the unique challenges and sacrifices that come with this profession, as well as the unpredictable path that life often takes.

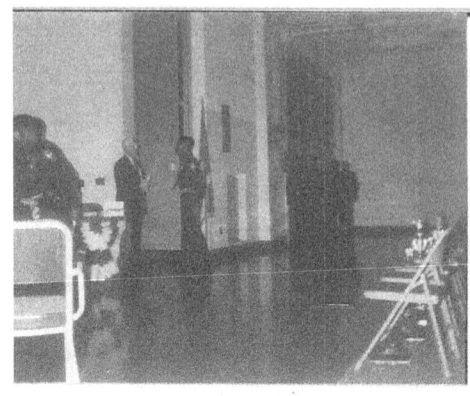

CHAPTER 3

District 1 - High Hopes
& A Hell of a Ride!

Before diving into the experiences that shaped my time as a new cadet in District 1, it's important to understand the role and responsibility of the *Field Training Officer (FTO)* in the *Field Training Officer Program*. The FTO plays a critical role in preparing rookie police officers or cadets for the realities of law enforcement. Ideally, the FTO is someone who has voluntarily stepped into the role – an officer with enough years of service to be confident, experienced, and knowledgeable in their job.

An FTO should also be someone with a genuine desire to teach and guide others. Unfortunately, this is not always the case. One of the worst scenarios for a rookie officer is to be assigned to an FTO who was coerced into the position, who lacks the proper qualifications, who has a massive ego or who thirsts for power and control over others. A trainer who doesn't want to train, or one who hasn't received the necessary preparation, can set a new officer on the wrong path from the beginning. Even worse, biases – whether personal, cultural, or racial – can influence the training dynamic and undermine the entire learning experience.

I believe I encountered a Field Training Officer who fell into one of these categories – racially biased, coerced, or possibly both. This made an already challenging transition from academy to real-world policing even harder!

Later in my career, I had the opportunity to step into the role of Field Training Officer myself. By then, I had developed a clear understanding of what was needed to make the FTO program successful and the impact it could have on a new officer's career. I trained (had assigned to me) three cadets during my time as an FTO: two females – one African American and the other Caucasian – and one Caucasian male. Other cadets were paired with me as training dictated or as needed. My goal was to ensure that each of them had an awesome, memorable, and enriching experience while learning how to perform their duties safely and effectively. I even permitted the male cadet's dad to ride along with us for a day.

I wanted them to leave their training with a sense of confidence, respect for the badge, and the tools necessary to succeed. It was my way of helping to shape the future of the department and ensuring that the next generation of officers would be well-prepared to serve the community with integrity. DPD also had a ride along program for Durham citizens. After they signed a waiver, they could ride with officers to acquire a better understanding of and an appreciation of what patrol officers do from day to day. I enjoyed this experience with my fellow Durhamites. I tried to make their experience one that they would not soon forget!

As for my first shift of duty, I remember reporting to District 1 substation, located in Wellon's Village, for my first shift of nighttime work. Walking into that substation for the first time was a moment I'll never forget. As I entered, I was greeted by the stares of the other officers present. Among the group, I noticed that I was one of two "Black" officers in a room with perhaps five white officers.

Having been subjected to racism in the past, I was already sensitive and alert to signs of discriminatory behavior. I admit that perhaps I had formed my own biases as a result of those experiences, but several of the white officers in the room struck me as "good old boys." Their demeanor, body language, and the unspoken tension in the room seemed to confirm my initial impression.

Not the least of these was my Field Training Officer (FTO), whose uniform was not well fitted, and to be frank, nothing about him gave the appearance that he was an officer. I would later come to the conclusion that he ranked on the lower level of these "good old boys," someone who seemed eager to prove himself as an officer but often fell short. His approach to training and interactions with me would eventually raise questions in my mind about his fitness for the role of FTO and whether he had truly embraced the responsibility of mentoring a rookie officer – or if he had been placed in the role reluctantly, without the necessary qualifications or the right mindset.

These initial impressions set the stage for my early days in District 1, where I would quickly come to understand the challenges and complexities of working in law enforcement, not only in the field but within the department itself.

State of North Carolina
Department of Justice

North Carolina Justice Academy

awards this

Certificate

to

Tony Lynn Scott

for satisfactory completion of the course in

Field Training Officer
(72 Hours)

this _____11th_____ day of _____July_____ , 19 __97__ .

_____
MICHAEL F. EASLEY, ATTORNEY GENERAL

_____
DIRECTOR

_____
COURSE COORDINATOR

First Shift: High Hopes and Growing Apprehension

I was excited about starting my first shift and eager to put my training into practice. Nevertheless, I couldn't ignore the great apprehension that came with it. Reporting to District 1 substation for that first night of work, I brought with me all the necessary tools for the job – my Cross pens, notepad, and other essentials to carry out my responsibilities as a new cadet.

The Field Training Officer (FTO) Program, if memory serves correctly, lasted for six months. During this time, my FTO was responsible for guiding me through the various facets of policing, ensuring I gained the skills and confidence necessary to patrol the streets of Durham independently. I began this phase of training with a sense of optimism and self-assurance, eager to learn and apply the lessons from the academy.

Early on in my training, my FTO had me communicating over the police radio – a task that can be intimidating for a rookie officer. While many of my academy classmates, who were assigned to other substations, had not yet been tasked with radio communication, my FTO had me using the radio much earlier than expected. I remember one or two of my academy peers reaching out to say, "Man, I heard you on the radio – you sound good." Their words of encouragement boosted my morale in those early days. One of these classmates was retired Sergeant Melvin Carter.

However, as training progressed, my relationship with my FTO took a turn for the worse; he was not the coach and encourager that he should have been. Instead, he became increasingly nitpicky over minor details as if he was looking to find some error – anything in my job performance, which I was being graded on. What should have been a constructive and supportive learning environment turned into a frustrating and, at times, demoralizing experience! His overly critical nature made each shift more difficult than it needed to be.

Rather than helping me refine my skills, his constant criticism began to chip away at my confidence. For the first time in my life, I felt myself doubting my abilities. It was an unfamiliar and deeply unsettling feeling! Each 12-hour shift, often spanning up to five consecutive days, became more of a burden than an opportunity. What had started as a hopeful and exciting experience quickly turned into a grueling ordeal – ***A Hell of a ride***, to say the least!

Looking back, I am reminded how much of my struggle during that time stemmed from my FTO's inability to effectively mentor and guide. Instead of being someone I could rely on to prepare me for the challenges of law enforcement, he became a source of unnecessary stress and frustration!

Relentless Anxiety and Tension

The anxiety and tension of riding with this Field Training Officer (FTO) were relentless. It never let up, and each shift felt heavier than the last. My confidence, which I had carried proudly from the academy, was shaken to its core. My grades began to slip, falling below the standard I knew I was capable of achieving. Looking back, I can't help but believe that this was part of his plan all along – to undermine me as a cadet and create the impression that I was incapable of doing the job.

That impression, however, couldn't have been further from the truth. I was fully capable, but the environment he created made it nearly impossible to thrive!

Fear and the Consequences of Leadership Failure

After completing the FTO phase and moving on, I learned more about this officer's reputation within the department. He was often ridiculed for being overly skittish and scared on the job. Officers who had worked with him told stories of how he was constantly and excitedly calling for backup, regardless of the situation. And when I say constantly, I mean *always!* I also witnessed this when I was no longer assigned to him… for years to come! No matter how routine the call, he seemed to lack the confidence to handle it independently.

He also had a habit of carrying his nightstick at all times as if it were a security blanket. This officer, who was supposed to train me in the skills and mindset of law enforcement, performed his duties in fear. And fear in the likes of what he demonstrated, as I later came to understand, is a dangerous trait for any officer to have!

As I matured in my career, I developed a philosophy that I often shared with fellow officers, especially those who struggled with fear when policing certain neighborhoods. I would tell them:

"If the day should come when you are afraid to police, you are a danger to yourself and others. That is the day you should leave the police department."

Fear compromises judgment, reactions, and decision-making. Policing is a profession that demands courage, composure, and the ability to face difficult situations head-on. To do otherwise puts everyone at risk — officers, civilians, and the community as a whole!

During my training, one member of my class came to this realization. Overwhelmed by fear during the FTO phase, they chose to leave the police department rather than continue in a role they couldn't handle safely. As difficult as it was to see them go, I respected their decision. It was better for them – and for the department – to step away than to try and force themselves into a role they were not equipped to manage.

A Potentially Deadly Encounter

By this point in my training with my Field Training Officer (FTO), we had moved from the District 1 substation in Wellon's Village to a new location on Main Street, almost directly across from the new police headquarters building. One day, during one of our shifts, we received a call regarding an individual walking down the street with a rifle in his hand. The call came in for an area between Liberty Street and Holloway Street, though the exact street name escapes me now.

We responded to the call and turned onto the street where the suspect had been reported. Sure enough, as we approached, we saw the individual walking toward us with the rifle clearly visible in his hand. The sight was jarring and immediately heightened the tension!

In the academy, we were taught a crucial lesson about firearms: **a long gun or rifle always has the advantage over a handgun!** With only our small .38 caliber handguns, the odds were certainly not in our favor should the situation escalate. I seem to recall that my FTO grabbed the shotgun that was assigned to us. This reality weighed heavily on me as we came to a stop!

I don't remember whether I was driving or my FTO at the time; however, I think it was him. What I do remember is the car stopping downhill and about 40 yards from the suspect who was facing us! My FTO exited the vehicle and, to my shock, ordered me to advance toward the individual holding the long gun. I followed the command, stepping out of the vehicle as we advanced toward the suspect!

Looking back, the gravity of the moment is undeniable. This could have easily turned into a consequential – and potentially deadly – encounter for both of us! We were in an incredibly vulnerable position, outgunned and uncertain of the individual's intent. The situation required careful judgment and coordination, but instead, I felt as though I was being thrown into the deep end with no guidance or support.

Fortunately, without incident, we were able to take the suspect into custody. As we were walking back to the car, I noticed that backup had arrived. I can't recall if they got there as we were advancing on the suspect or after we had already secured him, but our backup was none other than the other African American male officer I had seen on my first day reporting for duty. He was someone I had grown to admire and respect, a well-regarded and level-headed member of the squad.

I don't remember whether he spoke to both my FTO and me about what had just happened or whether he spoke to me alone, but he expressed disapproval about how the situation was handled. He emphasized the incredible danger and threat we had stepped into, advancing on a suspect armed with a rifle without waiting for sufficient backup. His words stuck with me and underscored what I had already been feeling about my FTO's decision-making.

This officer, however, would prove to be more than just a voice of wisdom in a tense moment. Over time, he became instrumental in my early career as a cadet, providing guidance and support that helped me navigate the challenges of my training and find my footing as a law enforcement officer.

A Lesson in Complacency

This is the second of the two incidents I previously mentioned involving my FTO. One day, during our shift, my FTO and I received a call to 505 W. Chapel Hill Street, which would eventually become the new headquarters building for the Durham Police Department. At the time, however, the building was vacant, and the call had come in because the alarm had been triggered.

It was broad daylight as we arrived on the scene, exited the vehicle, and began a walk around the building to ensure it was secure. Alarms going off in businesses throughout the city were not uncommon, but as a police officer, you could never treat a call as routine. Every call had to be approached as though danger might be lurking just around the corner. Complacency was a mistake you could never afford to make, and I understood that well, even as a cadet.

Nevertheless, unlike my FTO, I was not in the habit of grabbing my nightstick every time I exited the vehicle. As we conducted our perimeter check, my FTO noticed this and questioned me about it. He wanted to know why I wasn't carrying my nightstick.

Innocently and without giving it much thought, I responded that I believed I could handle the situation physically if needed to engage a potential suspect. I remind you, my readers, that we had received decent training in self-defense during the academy. My response to my FTO: "I had studied martial arts. I can, therefore, take care of myself." To me, the response felt straightforward and reasonable. But it quickly became clear that this was not the answer he wanted to hear.

His reaction, or the lack thereof, caused me to realize that he viewed the nightstick as an essential crutch, that clearly he depended on. I, on the other hand, believed that confidence in my physical ability, combined with my training, was sufficient to handle most situations. This difference in mindset only added to the growing tension between us and further highlighted the divide in how we approached the job. I will add that throughout my career, I never struck anyone with my nightstick or expandable baton when this became the replacement tool. I took great pride in being able to verbally de-escalate a situation or arrest a person with minimum force or the necessary force to conduct an arrest!

It wasn't long after the incident at 505 W. Chapel Hill Street that I found myself standing before the district commander who oversaw District 1 or the FTO program. I had no idea why I was being called to see the commander, but it quickly became clear. The first words out of his mouth – and the only thing I distinctly remember from that encounter – were: "So you don't want to carry your nightstick, and you know that martial arts stuff. I tell you, if you use that stuff against anyone, the department is not going to back you up."

His words hit me hard! I hadn't realized how much my response to my FTO during the building check had been twisted or blown out of proportion. I wasn't trying to reject protocol or suggest I didn't need to follow standard practices – I was simply answering a question based on my perspective at the time. But clearly, the situation had been reported in a way that cast doubt on my judgment and commitment to the department's expectations.

Not long after that meeting, my assignment with my current FTO was brought to an unexpected end. I don't recall the exact circumstances or what specific events led to the change, but I can only imagine that I was perceived as underperforming and on the verge of dismissal from the department.

In what may have been a final effort to salvage my training, I was reassigned to a different Field Training Officer. This new pairing would mark a turning point in my career – a chance to reset and prove my worth as a cadet in the department. I had performed well in the training academy, exceptionally well in comparison to others in my class. Perhaps the problems that I was reported as having were recognized as not me or my inability to do the job but instead my FTO. I would like to think this was the case.

A Reset: An African American FTO, What a Difference Maker

As stated, for the leading or exact reason(s) unbeknownst to me, I was reassigned to a new Field Training Officer. Perhaps it was, in fact, an effort to reset my training and salvage my career. Whatever the reason, this change turned out to be a pivotal moment!

My new FTO was the African American officer I had come to respect – the same one I saw on my first day reporting to work in District 1. His reputation for professionalism and level-headedness had preceded him, and I couldn't have asked for a better mentor at that time, if not the best within the police department; clearly one of the best!

Although I don't recall the details of our first conversation, I have no doubt that he worked to put me at ease. I imagine he addressed the difficulties I'd faced with my previous FTO and acknowledged how those experiences had worked against me. But what I do remember is his reassurance that this was a new start. He was committed to ensuring that I learned everything I needed to know to perform the job efficiently, thoroughly, and professionally!

Unlike my previous FTO, this officer exemplified what a Field Training Officer should be. His approach was one of guidance and encouragement, not criticism and intimidation. He didn't just tell me what to do – he showed me, coached me, and instilled in me the confidence I had lost along the way. This reset was exactly what I needed! It wasn't just about learning the mechanics of the job – it was about restoring my belief in myself and my ability to succeed as a law enforcement officer.

Being assigned to my new Field Training Officer was truly a breath of fresh air! Indeed, a new day had dawned, and I was excited to come to work and learn from such an experienced and professional mentor. His approach to training was not only effective but also enjoyable, making the experience of patrolling the streets of Durham something I looked forward to each day.

I remember being introduced to his family and friends while on patrol, including his mother, who was a local hairstylist. Those interactions added a personal touch to our workdays and gave me a glimpse into the community connections that shaped him as a person and an officer. His calm demeanor and ability to balance professionalism with approachability left a lasting impression on me.

Patrolling with him brought moments of excitement and real learning. I vividly recall a car chase that we were in that ended on the railroad tracks at Ramseur Street and Pettigrew St., near the old John Avery Boys Club. The suspect fled the vehicle, and a foot pursuit ensued. I remember jumping out of the car and instinctively taking off after the suspect, leaving my FTO behind. Afterward, he told me that as soon as I started running, he knew I was going to catch the person.

It wasn't long before it became a known fact around the department and throughout Durham: if you ran from Officer Scott, you were going to get caught! Somewhere along the way, from the community I served, I earned the nickname "Robocop," a title that has followed me for decades. Even now, nearly 40 years later, I occasionally run into someone who will call me by that name. Every time, I'm caught off guard, reminded of how far back it all goes.

My new FTO didn't just teach me the technical skills of law enforcement – he tested me in ways that pushed me to grow. His mentorship brought out the best in me, restoring my confidence and shaping my approach to the job in ways that would stick with me throughout my career.

Being assigned to this new Field Training Officer was truly refreshing. Indeed, a new day had dawned, and I was excited to come to work and learn from my FTO. His approach to training was not only effective but also engaging, making the experience of patrolling the streets of Durham something I looked forward to each day. The ways in which my FTO tested me varied, but they all served a purpose. He emphasized the importance of situational awareness and attention to detail, and the methods he used to test me truly sharpened my skills.

One way he tested me was by suddenly asking, "What street are you on?" This wasn't just a casual question – it was a critical safeguard! If something happened right in front of you, you needed to be able to quickly and accurately tell others where you were. Whether you needed backup or had to respond to a situation, knowing your exact location was vital to ensuring your safety and the safety of others. Back then, memorizing the streets in your district was a requirement. Unlike today, when GPS systems assist officers, we had to rely entirely on our knowledge of the area or paper maps when needed.

Another way he tested me was by pointing out potential suspicious activity during our patrols. On one occasion, we passed a car where the driver was holding a can. My FTO asked, "Did you see what that person was holding?" I was able to answer him correctly, identifying the can as a non-alcoholic beverage. It might seem like a small thing, but the exercise reinforced the importance of being observant and recognizing subtle details that could make a difference in the field.

He also quizzed me on my ability to recall people and situations. For instance, he might point out someone on the street and later ask me to describe what I saw. What was the person wearing? What were they doing? It was almost like playing a game, but it was serious business. These exercises were designed to develop my observational skills and ability to retain critical information under pressure.

His teaching style made learning fun, but the lessons themselves were invaluable. Under his guidance, I thrived! My confidence, which had been shaken during my initial FTO assignment, was restored. I learned to see the streets of Durham not just as places to patrol but as a landscape to be understood and navigated with precision. Unfortunately, another cadet, an African American who also had military training (he was a Lieutenant in the Air Force if my memory is correct), was assigned to my former FTO. I recall hearing from a co-worker that this cadet was ready to fight my previous FTO. Bad FTOs should be weeded out immediately when this becomes apparent. However, before I retired, I don't think the DPD was doing a good enough job with this. It doesn't help when a police department is understaffed; such was and currently is DPD over a decade later.

Eventually, I was released to patrol the streets of Durham on my own, within the same district where I had been trained - District 1. It was a moment of pride and accomplishment, and I knew I owed much of my growth and success to the thoughtful and thorough mentorship of my FTO (M.H.).

Inherent Dangers of Car-chasing

It was supposed to be a routine moment in my day. I was on duty but heading home for a quick lunch break as a C.O.P. officer. As I drove, I approached the intersection at Geer Street, having just exited Highway 70. Ahead of me was a city utility truck. The driver didn't come to a complete stop at the stop sign, but I wasn't planning to pull him over.

I was behind the truck southbound on Hardee Street, not giving it much thought until we reached Cheek Road. The driver then intentionally ran the red light! That caught my attention. I turned on my lights and sirens and called in the situation over the radio.

"Unit C-215 to communications. Vehicle failing to stop at traffic signals, we are southbound on Hardee Street. City utility truck, white."

What came next caught me off guard.

"Be advised: the suspect is wanted for escaping custody and has stolen a city vehicle. Exercise caution!"

I now understood the stakes. The driver wasn't just reckless; he was fleeing the law. I gave pursuit as he continued onto Raynor Street, blowing through stop signs and stop lights and speeding! I gave pursuit, slowing at intersections to ensure it was clear before continuing. By this point, the suspect had gained significant distance – at least two blocks ahead – continuing onto Liberty Street.

Using a parallel route, I managed to close the gap and regain visual contact. He was heading east, in the direction of downtown. The chase resumed as I rejoined directly behind him. At Driver Street, the suspect ran another stop sign and collided with a vehicle crossing the intersection. I stopped immediately to check on the other driver, who thankfully wasn't injured. Meanwhile, the suspect abandoned the utility truck and took off on foot, disappearing behind houses along Driver Street.

I relayed updates over the radio as I gave chase.

"Suspect is now fleeing on foot, south behind houses on Driver Street, heading toward Liberty."

Running hard in front of the houses on Driver Street, I kept him in sight, closing the gap. The foot chase spanned about two blocks. Finally, at the intersection of Driver and Liberty Street, I caught up to him. He was exhausted, out of breath, and had nowhere left to go. I secured him without further resistance and radioed in the apprehension.

As I sat in my patrol car, I got a call. It was my former field training officer (M.H.). His voice was calm but direct, exactly as I remembered from my training days. "Make sure you do everything by the book," he said. "Charge him with every infraction and every law he broke. And write up a thorough report."

Even after completing my training under him, he was still looking out for me. His words were a reminder to stay meticulous and professional. As I started the paperwork, I kept his advice in mind. It wasn't just about making the arrest; it was about doing the job right.

Drug, gun charges

Two men were arrested by Durham police officers on drug and weapons violations Thursday night on Wabash Street in McDougald Terrace.

Officers T.L. Scott and E.F. Mitchell arrested John Dwight Abrams of 807 Grant St. and a man who gave his name as Tony Jones, whose address was not available.

The officers stopped the two men in front of Building 13 on Wabash Street. They found a .38-caliber handgun in Jones' waistband and a .357-caliber handgun in Abrams' waistband. Both guns had been reported stolen. The officers also confiscated 17 bindles of crack cocaine.

Abrams and Jones were both charged with possession of crack cocaine with the intent to manufacture, sell or deliver, possession of a stolen firearm and carrying a concealed weapon.

Abrams was also charged with possession of a firearm by a convicted felon. Abrams was convicted of second-degree murder on June 22, 1988, and sentenced to 15 years in prison. He was paroled on Feb. 15, 1991. Abrams was convicted of the November 1986 slaying of Steven Bryant Wright, 30, of 817 Red Oak Ave., who was shot to death outside Frankie's Game Room at 933 E. Main St.

3 Charged With Drug Crimes

Durham Police Officer T.L. Scott was in two chases Monday and ended up charging three men with drug violations.

Scott said the first chase started about 3 p.m. in the parking lot of 2519 S. Roxboro St. when he saw a man drop a paper bag on the ground. Scott got the man's name and address and picked up the bag.

Scott said the man denied the bag was his and began to run. Scott chased the man through the Cornwallis Road housing project, but lost sight of him.

Scott charged the man, whose name was not revealed, with delaying and obstructing an officer and possession of cocaine with the intent to manufacture, sell or deliver. The paper bag contained four one-dose packets of cocaine.

About 3½ hours later officers received a call about drug dealing in front of the mailboxes at an apartment complex at 410 Pilot St.

Scott said that when he arrived he saw one man pass a packet of drugs to a second man.

The second man, identified as Otis Burnette of 410 Pilot St., ran into the woods behind 410 Pilot St. with Scott in pursuit.

Scott caught Burnette and scuffled with him before placing him under arrest. After he was arrested, Burnette was taken to Duke Hospital for treatment of dehydration.

Officer W.G. Johnson arrested the first man, Warren Goldston of 1312 Willowdaile Drive, in front of the mailboxes.

Goldston and Burnette were both charged with possession of cocaine with the intent to manufacture, sell and deliver. The packet contained two small bags of cocaine.

Burnette was also charged with delaying and obstructing an officer and robbery with a dangerous weapon. Scott said the warrant charged Burnette with robbing Darryl Lee of $100 on Aug. 25, 1987, by sticking a gun in his ribs and demanding money.

Goldston was also arrested on old warrants charging him with assault on a female and non-support.

Drug Arrests 11/10/89

Four people were arrested Friday night on drug charges after Durham police officers confiscated 27 bindles of cocaine near the basketball court in the McDougald Terrace housing project.

Dwayne Turrentine of 1314 South St., Antuan Smith of 620 Mimosa St., and Anthony Joyner of no known address were charged with felonious possession of cocaine and possession of cocaine with the intent to manufacture, sell or deliver. A 15-year-old was turned over to juvenile officers.

Officers found one bag containing five bindles of cocaine and a second bag containing 22 bindles of cocaine on a rock near the basketball court.

Man Faces Drug Charges

By KAMMIE MICHAEL
Herald staff writer

Steven Jerome Clark, 21, of 219 S. Alston Ave., Apt. A-9, was arrested Wednesday on drug charges after Durham police officers said they saw him place six bindles of cocaine in his mouth.

Officers T.L. Scott and M.B. Alston stopped Clark at Bacon and Lawson streets. When Clark saw the officers he stuffed the bags of cocaine in his mouth, Scott said.

Scott grabbed Clark's throat so he could not swallow and officers retrieved the bags of cocaine.

Clark was charged with felonious possession of cocaine with the intent to manufacture, sell or deliver. His bond was set at $5,000.

Man Faces Cocaine, Stolen Car Charges

George McFadden, 21, of 1506 S. Roxboro St. was arrested Friday night and charged with possession of a stolen car and possession of cocaine.

Durham Police Officer T.L. Scott saw a 1985 Toyota Camry on Roxboro Street near Moline Street about 11:30 p.m. that matched the description of a car reported stolen earlier Friday.

Scott stopped the car and discovered it was stolen.

He arrested McFadden, who was a passenger in the car, and the driver. Scott later released the driver after determining that she did not know the car was stolen.

When officers searched McFadden, they found two vials containing what appeared to be cocaine.

McFadden was also charged with two counts of failure to appear in court. He was placed in Durham County Jail in lieu of a $15,000 bond.

BLACK HISTORY MONTH

THE HERALD-SUN | PHOTOS BY CHRISTINE T. NGUYEN

Durham police officer Tony Scott reads a passage from "The Afro-American" to eighth-graders at Shepard Magnet Middle School on Friday as Qion Toney, 14, (right) looks at the late rap artist Tupac Shakur's "Rose That Grew From The Concrete." The school held an African-American Read-In Day on Friday, in which community leaders read poems, historical books and autobiographies along with Shepard students.

Cash taken from store

Ricky Lewis Kornegay, 28, of 31-F Lawson St., was arrested Friday night and charged with stealing $126 from a cash register at the Town 'n Country convenience store on Lawson Street.

A clerk told officers that two men came in the store about 6:30 p.m. Friday. One man reached in the register and grabbed a handful of bills while employees were distracted by the second man.

Officer T.L. Scott found Kornegay asleep inside a van a short time later. Officers found money in Kornegay's shoes.

Kornegay was charged with common-law robbery.

Police *From 1C*

Bond for Civers was set at $30,000.

Stolen Motorcycle Nets Arrest

Clifton Jones of 2015 Athens Ave. was arrested for possession of a stolen motorcycle and traffic violations after a chase Wednesday near the McDougald Terrace housing project.

Officer T.L. Scott tried to stop the motorcycle, it sped off on Sima Street. Scott chased it to Rosewood Avenue, where the driver cut through several yards.

Scott pulled into a driveway and the motorcycle struck his patrol car. The cyclist jumped off and ran behind a house, where Scott caught him.

The motorcycle was reported stolen Tuesday from 511 Gattis St.

CHAPTER 4

A Rising Sentinel: The Go-Getter, but Hold on a Minute

Having successfully completed the Field Training Officer Program under my new FTO, I was now released to patrol the streets of Durham on my own as a rookie police officer. While this was a significant milestone, I was still considered a cadet in training and remained on probation for, I believe was, six months. Each day I reported to work, I performed my duties just as they were required of every other officer – no exceptions.

My responsibilities included answering calls for service, providing police advice, writing incident reports, investigating traffic accidents, and carrying out all the tasks that came with the job. There was no hand-holding, no special treatment. The expectations were clear, and I embraced them with enthusiasm. These were indeed exciting times, filled with new experiences and opportunities to prove myself.

A New Era of Policing

During this season of policing, and even before being released from the academy to patrol on my own, we were made aware of a growing crisis:

the emergence and spread of crack cocaine. While in the police academy, we were told about the havoc the drug was wreaking on the West Coast. Stories of addiction, violence, and community devastation were already making headlines, and it was clear that this epidemic was not going to stay confined to one region.

With each passing year, crack cocaine made its way eastward, and Durham was not immune to its effects!. The Bull City began to experience the ripple effects of this destructive drug, and it became evident that law enforcement would be on the front lines of a new and challenging battle. As a young officer, I couldn't yet fully grasp the magnitude of the storm that was approaching, but I knew that the work we were doing would soon take on an even greater level of complexity and urgency.

Before the rampant spread and takeover of crack cocaine on the streets of Durham, the city was known for the prevalence of a different drug: heroin. In particular, one location – Canal Street – stood out as a hotspot where heroin could be readily purchased. Heroin had a noticeably different effect on its users compared to crack cocaine. The drug was more subduing, leaving its users in a lethargic state and often altering their mental state in a way that subdued their behavior. It created a quieter, though equally destructive, kind of addiction.

Crack cocaine, on the other hand, was a completely different animal. When it began to spread through Durham, it brought a new kind of energy and devastation to the community! Unlike the sedative effects of heroin, crack cocaine provided an intense high – a rush of exhilaration that its users desperately sought to recapture each time they used the drug. From what I learned during my time on the streets, that first high was like no other! It was said to be so powerful that users would chase it endlessly, though they could never quite regain the initial experience.

One individual I spoke with described crack cocaine in startling terms. They told me that the drug, for them, was "better than sex!" Can you imagine that kind of comparison? It was a testament to the drug's grip on its users, a grip so strong that it could alter even the most primal human instincts.

As crack cocaine spread, the landscape of policing in Durham began to shift. The drug didn't just affect its users – it affected families, neighborhoods, and the very fabric of the community. For law enforcement, it was clear that we were entering a new era of challenges, one that would demand a different level of vigilance, strategy, and resolve.

The Rise of Crack Cocaine and Its Impact

As I patrolled the streets of Durham, I began to make arrests involving individuals who had heroin in their possession. However, it wouldn't be long before heroin was largely replaced by crack cocaine. This shift didn't just change the type of drug being used – it reshaped the very character of The Bull City!

As crack cocaine swept across Durham, it mirrored the devastating effects it was having on other major cities and small towns throughout the country. This drug was unlike anything we had seen before. Highly addictive and widely available, it tore through communities, leaving destruction in its wake!

The impact was immediate and far-reaching! Gun violence increased! Theft increased! The crime rate skyrocketed! Neighborhoods that had once been stable began to unravel under the weight of addiction and criminal activity. Families were torn apart as loved ones fell victim to the drug's grip, and entire communities were transformed into battlegrounds.

But crack cocaine didn't just devastate the individuals and families it touched directly – it also brought new and dangerous elements into the community. Individuals from other cities, states, and even neighboring islands began infiltrating Durham to establish a foothold in the local drug trade. These outsiders didn't come to be part of the community – they came to claim and control territory!

This led to territorial disputes and turf wars, which brought even more violence to the streets. These conflicts became the norm throughout the country, wherever crack cocaine had established its presence. For officers like me patrolling the streets, it was clear that this wasn't just about drugs – it was about a systemic shift in the dynamics of crime, safety, and community life.

Recognized as a Go-Getter

While working in District 1, I had developed a reputation as a go-getter, both among my colleagues and the residents of the communities I patrolled. It was well-known that if you ran from Officer Scott – better known by my nickname, "Robocop" – you were going to get caught.

One particular incident stands out to me, one that took place in Few Gardens early one morning. As I patrolled the area, I noticed an individual walking near the neighborhood. I recognized him immediately as a habitual shoplifter and known drug user. As I drove past him, I observed him deliberately shift his hand, clearly attempting to conceal whatever he was holding.

I circled the block to engage him, but as I approached, he took off running. A foot chase ensued, and this one would turn out to be unlike any other I had experienced. We left the main street surrounding Few Gardens and ran deep into the neighborhood itself. At one point, we found ourselves circling around and around a parked car. It felt like an endless game of cat and mouse, with my exhaustion mounting by the second.

I remember thinking, "Please let him stop soon!" Thankfully, he did. Eventually, he came to a halt, and I was able to make the arrest without further incident. This chase, though tiring, was a reminder of the unpredictable nature of law enforcement. You never knew when a routine patrol might turn into a test of endurance and determination. For me, it was also a reflection of the commitment I brought to the job – a refusal to give up, no matter the challenge.

The Foot Chase That Got Away

There is one last foot chase that I want to recall, and I'm quite certain it was the only one I ever "lost," if I may call it that. This incident also took place in Few Gardens, and it was a lesson I wouldn't soon forget.

As law enforcement officers, we are trained to exercise caution when chasing a suspect, particularly when approaching corners. We are taught to widen our angle when turning corners to avoid being caught off guard by a suspect who might be lying in wait. During this particular chase, there were three corners I had to navigate. As I approached the third corner, I followed my training, widening my angle to ensure I wouldn't be surprised. However, when I turned that last corner, the suspect I had been pursuing had completely vanished!

I stood there momentarily stunned, wondering where he could have gone. There was no logical place for him to hide, and he hadn't been running fast enough to completely disappear. Then it dawned on me – this individual had done what many suspects would resort to when desperate: he had run, without invitation, into someone's home!

This was a first for me and a stark reminder of the lengths people would go to in their attempts to evade capture. Though I didn't catch the suspect that day, the experience reinforced the unpredictable nature of the job and the need to remain vigilant at all times!

Concluding My Time as a Cadet in District 1: But Hold on a Minute

I will now conclude my experience as a cadet while in District 1, still under the watchful eye of my FTO and our sergeant, a Caucasian individual. Two particular incidents involving this supervisor stand out vividly in my memory and serve as a fitting close to my time in District 1.

The incident began when my supervisor became involved in a car chase. I happened to be near him at the time and quickly joined the pursuit. This chase took place in an area where the Durham Bulls baseball field now stands. The street (Dillard) where it occurred no longer exists, but I remember it clearly – a steep downhill road that led to an eventual crash!

The suspect, driving the vehicle, lost control and crashed into the side of the old tobacco factory. I was closely behind my supervisor as we approached the scene. The suspect jumped and ran from the vehicle, but what my supervisor did next completely caught me off guard! As he exited his vehicle, still communicating the chase over his handheld radio, my supervisor did something that left me dumbfounded. To my utter surprise, he threw his radio at the fleeing suspect... But hold on a minute! The act made absolutely no sense to me! I stood there, momentarily frozen, trying to process what I had just witnessed.

It seemed to me that his actions were fueled by frustration – perhaps because the suspect, an African American man, had successfully evaded him. Whatever his reasoning, this was unreasonable, unnecessary and unprofessional, leaving me questioning his judgment in the heat of the moment.

The second incident involving my Caucasian supervisor left me more dumbfounded than when he threw his radio. The details of what took place are sketchy now, but I believe I may have been serving a warrant on an individual when the situation unfolded. We were on Hyde Park Street near Juniper Street, in a predominantly African American community. I had escorted the individual to the hood of my police car and was in the process of attempting to handcuff him. My supervisor, who had checked in with me, stood nearby watching the interaction.

As I tried to secure the handcuffs, the individual began to resist. This forced me to elevate my use of force to gain control over the situation. In the course of restraining him, his head struck the side of the windshield, causing a gash near his eye.

What happened next took me by surprise. My supervisor looked at me and simply said, "Good job, good job!" I remember being stunned by his response… But hold on a minute! What was "good" about what had just happened? Was he commending me for manhandling this individual? For me, this wasn't a "good job," as he seemed to suggest – it was a necessary job.

Unfortunately, the man required medical care as a result of the injury he sustained. My supervisor, however, appeared completely unconcerned with that fact. His reaction seemed more rooted in satisfaction that I had responded with what he deemed appropriate force.

This incident left a bitter taste in my mouth. It underscored the differences in how we viewed policing, especially in situations involving force. For me, law enforcement was about doing what was necessary to maintain control while ensuring that everyone involved – including those being arrested – was treated with respect and care. My supervisor's lack of concern for the man's well-being and his eagerness to applaud my actions felt misguided and troubling. The arrestee received medical attention at the scene before being transported to the M.O. – Magistrate's Office for processing into the jailing facility.

The Influence of Leadership and Culture

What I experienced with my Caucasian supervisor – the lack of respect or concern for the well-being of others – was not unique to him as an individual. Unfortunately, this kind of indifference could manifest in any officer, regardless of ethnicity. It often stemmed from the tone and behavior set by the supervisor or the strong-minded leader of a squad.

A supervisor's attitude and actions can shape the culture of their team. When a supervisor acts unprofessionally, it becomes easier – and sometimes even expected – for those under their leadership to follow suit. A culture of misconduct or indifference doesn't arise from isolated incidents; it develops over time and thrives in environments where there is little accountability or oversight.

I know firsthand what it's like to speak out against wrongdoing, only to become ostracized and targeted by leadership as a result. The fear of retaliation is real, and the consequences can be isolating and severe. This is an experience I will share soon enough when I begin to recount my time as a C.A.T. Team member.

At the time, four decades ago, there was no official "code of silence," but the reality of the job often created an unspoken expectation of loyalty. Your life depended on the officers you worked with, and speaking out against them could lead to isolation, lack of backup, or even jeopardizing your job. The stakes were high, and the consequences of challenging a problematic culture were significant!

It was also an era when citizen complaints were largely dismissed. People's voices weren't often heard, even when complaints were clearly necessary. Without accountability, the wrong behaviors of a few officers could influence the entire squad, creating a domino effect that perpetuates misconduct.

When you see multiple officers engaging in wrongdoing, it's almost never an isolated or random occurrence. It is often the result of a culture that has been allowed to fester, shaped by leadership that either turned a blind eye or actively encouraged it. This isn't to say every officer conformed to these behaviors, but the environment made it difficult to act otherwise without fear of retaliation or ostracism.

These experiences taught me an important lesson about the power of leadership and the responsibility it carries. A supervisor who sets the right example can inspire professionalism and integrity, but one who leads poorly can create a dangerous and toxic culture.

CHAPTER 5

Sleepeth No More: Growth & Change Within the Bull City

From the time I was released from the academy to patrol the streets of Durham on my own, from 1988 to approximately 1995, the city of Durham, for the most part, was beginning to go to sleep after 6 o'clock pm. Even on Friday and Saturday nights – party nights, the city would settle into a lull around 1 a.m., leaving the streets quiet and uneventful.

During those early years, it was not unusual for me to patrol the streets from 1 a.m. to 5:45 a.m. with little more than my own thoughts to occupy the time. Police calls were few and far between, and the silence on the radio was so constant that I'd often click the mic just to ensure it was still working. Durham, as a city, was at rest – but this was all about to change!

In 1995, the opening of the Durham Bulls Ballpark marked the beginning of a transformation. The city began to stir from its slumber. Downtown Durham saw a surge of new energy as businesses started to take on a different look and purpose. Then, around 2005, the renovation of the Tobacco Warehouse District further awakened Durham, giving the city a new look and feel. It was as though Durham had shed its quiet past and stepped boldly into a new era.

Changes Within the Durham Police Department

As the city evolved, so too did the Durham Police Department. One of the most significant catalysts for change within the department was the leadership of Chief Trevor Hampton. When he came on board, he brought fresh vision and ushered in a wave of new equipment and practices.

Under his leadership, I believe we transitioned from three-channel radios to multi-channel radios, allowing us to communicate with other agencies – a crucial upgrade that improved coordination and response times. We also moved from the outdated .38 caliber handgun to the more efficient semi-automatic handgun, a change that enhanced officer readiness in the field.

Over time, other equipment was introduced as well:

- Mace, which added a non-lethal option for handling combative situations.

- Expandable batons, replacing the older, less versatile nightsticks and the Taser.

- Beepers, which allowed for better communication, though they were soon replaced by bag phones and later cell phones.

These advancements weren't just about modernization; they represented a department adapting to meet the growing challenges of the job.

Growth in the Streets

While the city and the department experienced positive growth, the streets of Durham saw a far more troubling kind of growth. The spread of crack cocaine continued to plague neighborhoods, with crack cocaine fueling addiction, crime, and violence.

Adding to the problem, gangs began to infiltrate the community, bringing a new level of organized crime and territorial disputes. The once-quiet streets I had patrolled in the late-night hours were now more active, and not in a good way. The influx of gangs created new challenges for law enforcement and further disrupted the fabric of the community.

Durham had changed. It was no longer the sleepy city I had first encountered as a rookie officer. While there was much to celebrate in terms of progress and development, the darker realities of crime and addiction loomed large, shaping the way we policed and the way the city lived.

The Expansion of Durham and Its Districts

With the growth of the City of Durham, the boundaries of the districts expanded as well. I distinctly remember how District 1, to the north, stretched further than before. What once ended near the Gear Street area expanded by approximately two miles to include East Club Blvd. This expansion wasn't unique to District 1. Across the city, each of the four original districts grew to accommodate Durham's rapid development.

In addition to the expansion of the original districts, a **fifth district** – the Downtown District – was established. This was a direct result of the city's transformation. Downtown Durham was no longer the quiet, sleepy area I had patrolled in my early years. It had become a bustling hub of activity, driven by new businesses, renovated spaces, and a growing nightlife.

Downtown Durham no longer went to sleep after 5pm, where it was all but empty – a ghost town feel, with the exception of the homeless.

The Distinct Characteristics of Each District

Each district within Durham had its own unique character, shaped by the people, businesses, and challenges that defined it.

- **District 1 (East Durham):**

  District 1 had its own set of challenges, particularly because it included a significant number of low-income neighborhoods. Areas like Few Gardens and another public housing complex off Highway 98 were part of this district, and these communities often required a higher police presence. At the time, District 1 saw a disproportionate amount of crime compared to other districts, which kept officers consistently busy and on high alert! Earlier, I mentioned Canal St. and the availability of Heroin from this location. Yes, this street is in District 1. I recall a startling incident that occurred in the housing development off Hwy 98 / Holloway St. I was sitting in my patrol car at Lynn Rd and Holloway Street while talking to another officer who had pulled. We heard shots rang out from the neighbor. He went into the neighborhood from one direction and I from the other. We both encountered the suspect with the gun; he was immediately taken into custody. The victim, a female, had been shot two or three times – once in the face and hand. She was obviously in shock and pain. However, she would survive this incident.

Project BABES, Bodies Are Beautiful, held a workshop recently to help youth focus on good health. They try to encourage a healthy lifestyle for a better life. (Photo by Lawson)

MONDAY, APRIL 4, 1988

Boyfriend shoots woman in mouth, both hands

Sheilah Louise Minor of Durham, shot yesterday in the mouth and both hands during an apparent quarrel with her boyfriend, was in fair condition in intensive care today at Durham County General Hospital.

Ronald Jerome Bell, 38, of 3040 Wedgedale Drive, was arrested in the shooting.

Durham police officers T.L. Scott and R.T. Chappell were parked near Bell's home and heard shots. They arrived seconds later, finding Ms. Minor, of 2412 Vesson Ave., Apt. 6, lying wounded in the front yard of a house on Wedgedale Drive. A man with a gun was standing next to her.

Durham police detective K.J.

Naylon said Ms. Minor was Bell's girlfriend. The two apparently began quarreling inside Bell's house, where several shots were fired. More shots were fired as Bell chased Ms. Minor outside, Naylon said.

The bullet that struck Ms. Minor's mouth lodged in her neck near the carotid artery, Naylon said. She also was wounded in the left hand and right index finger.

Officers arrested Bell and took a .25-caliber automatic pistol from him. Bell was charged with assault with a deadly weapon with intent to kill, inflicting serious bodily injury. He was placed in Durham County Jail under $50,000 bond.

- **District 2 (Northern Durham):**

District 2 was predominantly a middle-class area. While it did include some government housing neighborhoods, it also had a significant number of businesses and major roads, including Hwy 85, which made it busy in a different way. Officers in District 2 often dealt with the challenges of traffic accidents and business-related incidents, which required a great deal of report writing. Violent Crime existed here, too, of course, but it wasn't as prevalent as in District 1.

- **District 3 (West Durham):**

District 3 also had its share of businesses and major roadways, making it another area where officers were tasked with a lot of administrative work related to business incidents and accidents. However, like the other districts, District 3 had its government housing neighborhoods and low-income neighborhoods, which presented its own set of challenges.

- **District 4 (Southern Durham):**

District 4, in many ways, mirrored District 1. It had its public housing neighborhoods and low-income areas, and officers here dealt with a higher volume of crime, similar to those in East Durham. The challenges of policing throughout the city were rooted in the socioeconomic struggles faced by many of its residents, which were fueled by *Gentrification and Urban Renewal.* From my observations alone, Districts 4 and 1 were more directly affected by these two land grabs!

The City That No Longer Slept

By this time, Durham was no longer a quiet city. The once-muted police radio had become more active, reflecting the growing complexity of the city and its districts. Each area had its own unique demands, but they all shared a common thread: the need for dedicated officers who could adapt to the city's rapid growth and the challenges that came with it.

Meeting the Challenges of a Growing City

As Durham continued to grow, the Durham Police Department worked to address the city's unique challenges by expanding its resources and creating specialized units as needed. Among these additions were the motorcycle unit and the TA.C.T. unit, which were tasked with patrolling the major highways throughout Durham, with the motorcycle unit being essentially assigned to the downtown area along with the Bicycle Squad. The T.A.C.T units handled the investigation of major traffic accidents, particularly those involving fatalities, as well as patrolling Durham's Highways. Their presence on the highways was vital to ensuring safety and responding to critical incidents with precision and expertise.

In the early to mid-1990s, the department also collaborated with state and federal agencies through joint task forces to combat the growing issues of drugs, gangs, and violence that plagued the city. As the late 1990s approached, the gang unit was established to specifically address the infiltration of gangs into Durham. These gangs brought new challenges, including territorial disputes and increased violence.

Another key initiative during this period was the formation of the **C.A.T. Team (Crime Area Target Team)** in the early 1990s. This unit was specifically created to tackle the crack epidemic that was sweeping through Durham. I was a member of the C.A.T. Team, but I'll share more about those experiences later.

By this time, Durham had grown so rapidly and become so busy that the city no longer slept. Calls for service came in around the clock, and the radio traffic reflected the nonstop demands on officers.

In those days, there was a specific 10-code… "10 7 code-1" – that officers used to signal a request for a lunch break. However, as the city's activity increased, the ability to call out for lunch all but disappeared. Officers had to learn to eat their meals whenever and wherever they could, often grabbing a bite in between calls. The sheer volume of work and the unrelenting pace of the job made it clear that Durham was no longer the quiet city it had once been.

A Strain on Resources

The rapid growth of the city created a strain on police resources. The department's staffing levels struggled to keep up with the increased demands of patrolling a busy and expanding Durham. This shortage of officers often meant that units were stretched thin, sometimes covering multiple districts at once.

I recall one particular incident that occurred while I was assigned to District 4, which covered the southern part of Durham. I received a call that required me to travel all the way across town to District 2, located in the northern part of the city. I believe it was a disturbance call, but what stood out to me wasn't the nature of the call – it was the distance I had to travel and the fact that there were no closer units available to respond.

Out of concern, I called my wife while making the journey. I shared my worries about the shortage of officers and the risk involved in such a situation. I informed her, "If something happens to me, retain an attorney and find out whether or not there was sufficient backup available." The lack of available officers created a constant sense of unease, as every call carried the risk of being outnumbered or unsupported!

Now, more than 10 years into retirement, I believe this issue still persists. Retaining enough officers to adequately patrol the busy streets of Durham has remained a challenge despite the city's continued growth and the increasing demands placed on law enforcement. It does not help that there are those unreasonable people who are talking about *defunding the police!* Nevertheless, there have been too many incidents involving officer who either abused their authority or committed criminal acts while working in the communities they were sworn to protect and serve. These matters and others have worked against adequately staffing larger police departments.

CHAPTER 6

A Sentinel to District 4 & Beyond

During my 27 years of policing, I had the opportunity to work in each district. As I've mentioned, each district had its similarities and distinctions, but certain situations – like homicides and suicides – were universal, touching every corner of the city. While I will share some of my experiences in District 4, I want to first share two suicide cases from other districts that left lasting impressions on me. These tragic situations, though common in law enforcement, serve as a sobering reminder of the depths of despair some individuals face.

The Male Student

The first incident involved a male student from one of the local universities. For reasons I will never know, he chose to end his life through hanging. Arriving on the scene was a somber experience. It was clear that his pain, though invisible to others, had consumed him to the point of no return. While this particular case didn't linger with me as vividly as others, the loss of such a young life was no less heartbreaking!

The Female Student

The second incident, involving a female student from another local university, left an indelible mark on me! The memory of that scene was like a photograph taken with a flash camera – burned into my mind, lingering for days, if not weeks, after the fact.

This young woman had clearly planned out her actions. When we arrived on the scene, the situation was strikingly vivid. She had half filled a bathtub with water, unclothed herself, and entered the tub, where she took her life with a weapon. The image of her lifeless body in the water stayed with me., flashing through my mind like a haunting memory!

It was a stark reminder of the silent battles people fight and the tragic losses that result when those battles are lost. As officers, we are called to these scenes, often witnessing the aftermath of unimaginable pain. And while we strive to maintain our composure and professionalism, the emotional weight of these moments is impossible to ignore.

The Impact

Each suicide call I responded to left a mark, but the female student's case stood out for its graphic detail and the profound sadness it carried. The weight of such moments is one of the hidden burdens of law enforcement. While officers are trained to handle traumatic situations, there are some images and experiences that remain with you long after the scene is cleared.

Grateful for What I Didn't Encounter

As mentioned, during my time as a police officer, I responded to numerous graphic scenes and took reports of deeply disturbing situations.

The job often brought me face-to-face with the harsh realities of human suffering and tragedy.

However, I was fortunate enough to never have to deal with a situation that involved the victimization of a child or the death of a child. These are some of the most heartbreaking cases that officers can encounter, and I count myself truly grateful that I was spared from witnessing such pain firsthand. This is not to say the job wasn't emotionally taxing, but the absence of these particular experiences is something I have always been thankful for.

That said, engaging with children was one of the funnest and most rewarding things that can be done within the community. Some young people were afraid of the police officers, and I enjoyed working with the kids so they would not be afraid. I would have police stickers for them, and I would let them talk on the PA system or turn on the siren just to develop a rapport with the kids in the neighborhood. This was always an exciting time for them, as well as an exciting time for me! The relationship officers develop with kids will stay with them for a lifetime. Our interaction within their communities with their parents and others also will influence them. Where there are kids involved or present, law enforcement officers must be extra careful regarding how they conduct themselves among kids.

For these reasons, it's critical that law enforcement officers conduct themselves with care and professionalism when children are present. Kids are always watching, and the experiences they have with police officers – positive or negative – will influence their perceptions for years to come.

For me, those moments of connection with kids were more than just fun; they were an opportunity to show them that police officers are there to protect and serve, not to intimidate or harm. These interactions reminded me of the power we have to shape the future by building trust and fostering positive relationships, one child at a time.

A Night to Remember: Rescuing Tyrone P.

There was one situation involving a child – an infant, in fact – that could have ended disastrously but instead turned into one of the most memorable and rewarding moments of my career. At the time, I was a three-year veteran with the Durham Police Department and assigned to District 4.

It was a rainy night, and I was somewhere near the Cornwallis Projects on Roxboro Road when a call came out. A vehicle had been stolen from a local service station located at the corner of Roxboro Road and Cornwallis Road. Adding urgency to the situation, the report stated that there was a child in the car!

I was seconds behind the vehicle, though I never had it in sight. I proceeded down Archdale Road, following the direction in which the car was reported to have traveled. To my utter surprise, I eventually spotted the taillights of the vehicle. The car had crashed down a 15-foot embankment into a creek. Water from the creek, swollen by the rain, was beginning to flood and engulf the inside of the car.

Arriving at the scene, the suspect was nowhere to be found, but the child was still inside the vehicle. Without hesitation, I entered the waterlogged car, reached the child secured in the car seat, and rescued him! I handed the infant to a fellow officer who was standing outside the vehicle on the embankment. This officer, whose name I no longer recall, received the child from my hands.

The child's name, Tyrone P., stayed with me for two reasons. First, it was mentioned in a news article covering the incident, which I still have; secondly, years later, after my retirement, Tyrone – or someone close to him – recognized me on Facebook. Tyrone reached out to me via Facebook. He said that his mom had shared with him the story of that rainy night when I rescued him.

Reconnecting with Tyrone after so many years was an incredible experience! It was a reminder of how one moment of action can have a lasting impact on someone's life. That rainy night, which could have ended in tragedy, turned out to be one of the proudest and most fulfilling evenings of my career. As a result of my actions on that night, I received an award for *"High Levels of Professionalism."* Additionally, I received the *Officer of the Month Award* at least twice and additional recognitions for my service to *The Bull City* over my career.

Durham baby plucked from stolen car in creek

By JANE STANCILL
Correspondent

DURHAM — Officers rushing to the scene of an accident involving a stolen car arrived early Thursday to find the vehicle half-submerged in a rain-swollen creek.

They also heard the sound of a baby crying.

In the predawn darkness, Officer T.L. Scott reached into the back seat, which was two-thirds full of cold water, and plucked the 9-month-old boy from a child safety seat.

"The water was coming up to the baby's chest, and it was still rising," Officer Scott said in an interview later Thursday. "If he had not been in the child seat, I am more than convinced he would have drowned."

The rescue ended a wild series of events during which the infant's mother had been assaulted, her car had been stolen, and the assailant had driven the car down a 15-foot embankment and smashed it into a creek — with 9-month-old Tirone D. Peace in the back.

Police described what happened this way:

About 4 a.m., Felichia M. Peace of Durham stopped at the Buy Quick Food Mart on West Corn-

> **'I just reacted when I heard the baby crying. I automatically went to the car and did what I had to do.'**
>
> — Officer T.L. Scott

wallis Road to phone her father and ask him to unlock the door for her. Because it was raining heavily, she had left Tirone strapped into his infant seat in her 1980 Mercury.

As she was talking a pay phone, a man grabbed her from behind and hung up the phone. The man — described as a slender black man with a light beard — threatened her with a gun and tried to drag her in a headlock behind the store.

But Ms. Peace managed to grab a bottle from atop an ice machine and hit him in the head. She broke free and ran into the street, where she hoped to flag down a passerby.

The assailant chased her into the street and ripped off her shirt before she could get away to a nearby house, where she called police.

When Ms. Peace came outside to wait for police she saw a

terrifying sight — her car, with her son inside, was missing from the front of the store.

As police raced to the scene, they got a second call — a report of an accident on South Roxboro Street at Archdale Street, about a quarter of a mile from the store.

When officers Scott and J.D. Martin arrived, they found Ms. Peace's car half-submerged in six feet water at the bottom of a 15-foot embankment. The car apparently had skidded off the road at a sharp curve and skidded 100 feet before hitting the creek. The horn had been set off, and officers heard the sound of a baby crying. The suspect was nowhere in sight.

Officer Scott said he had little time to think. "I just reacted when I heard the baby crying," he said. "I automatically went to the car and did what I had to do."

Ms. Peace was reunited with her son as emergency medical technicians examined him on the scene. Although her car was a total loss, the baby was not hurt.

"I thought they were going to say something else when they found my baby," she said. "But they told me what I wanted to hear. Lord, I was so glad to get him back.

"They got him out just in time, thank goodness."

3 Arrested After Chases That Ends On NCCU Campus

Three men were arrested and warrants have been issued for a fourth after a chase Tuesday evening that ended on the campus of N.C. Central University.

Troy Lee Howard, 24, of 601 Elm St., Otis Lee Burnette of 3812 Missile St., and Reginald

2 Charged In Robbery
Of Off-Duty Cab Driver

Two men were arrested early Tuesday and charged with robbing Tony Sampson at gunpoint in front of Sampson's apartment on Pilot Street.

Keith Oliver Austin, 17, of 406 Cecil St., and Brian Alexander Scott, 19, of 2109 Otis St., were each charged with robbery with

Dale Leathers, 28, of 3817 Dunn St., were each arrested and charged with delaying and obstructing an officer.

Warrants were issued for Leathers' brother, Bobby Lee Leathers Jr., charging him with speeding to elude an officer, careless and reckless driving, failure to stop for blue lights and siren and two stop sign violations. Leathers had not been arrested by late Tuesday.

The chase started about 8 p.m. when Durham Police Officers M.L. Hayes and Tony Scott saw a man running from the corner of Main and Elm Street toward a car. As the officers approached the car from Angier Avenue, the car went through a stop sign and sped off, Hayes said.

The officers chased the car

onto Ramseur Street and then across the railroad tracks to Grant Street. The car turned on to Lincoln Street and then onto Lawson Street.

Hayes and Scott chased the car onto the NCCU campus near Pearson Cafeteria, where the four men in the car jumped out and ran.

Hayes caught Howard and Scott caught Reginald Leathers near the NCCU music building.

An off-duty police officer, Tommie Clark, was riding a bicycle toward the NCCU campus on Fayetteville Street when he saw Burnette running down the street. Clark jumped off his bicycle and chased Burnette to the front of Number 4 Fire Station on Fayetteville Street, where he made the arrest.

PAGE 2C   DURHAM MORNING HERALD   THURSDAY, NOVEMBER 23, 1980

Saving Children Earns Accolades For Three Police Officers

By KAMMIE MICHAEL
Herald staff writer

Three Durham police officers were honored Monday for showing "high levels of professionalism" in the performance of their duties during the past three months.

All three officers — M.E. Harris, T.L. Scott and J.L. Wood — earned their awards for their handling of incidents involving babies. The officers were the first recipients of the awards given by the Fraternal Order of Police, Lodge Number 2.

• Wood, a 15-year veteran of the department, was commended for his actions on Sept. 16 when he chased a stolen car with the owner's small child inside.

The car, which contained 14-year-old Amber Nicole Bell of Rothway Drive, was stolen from a business on Guess Road while the child's mother dropped off lunch to her husband.

Wood spotted the car on Knox Street at Roxboro Road. He said he had to weigh the dangers of a chase against the need to get the child back to her parents.

"When I got behind him I wasn't going to chase the car. I was just going to follow him," Wood said.

The driver, Leary Henry Wood of R1 1, New Hill, drove through the middle of two lanes of cars on Mangum Street and tried to get away from Wood.

"Then I had to go ahead and chase him because I did not know what plans he had for the baby," Wood said. "I didn't want a high-speed chase, but I couldn't let him get away either."

The chase ended on Liberty Street at Alston Avenue when Leater Wood crashed his car into the back of a car stopped for the traffic light.

The child suffered a gash on her forehead.

"After the accident, she wasn't crying. I was riding her on my

shoulder," Wood said. "She started to cry when the ambulance people came."

• Scott, a three-year police veteran, was honored for rescuing a 9-month-old baby from a wrecked car which landed in a rain-swollen creek on Oct. 19.

The baby, Tyrone Peace of Oak Ridge Boulevard, was made his mother's car when it was stolen from outside the Buy Quick convenience store on South Roxboro Street about 4 a.m.

"I drove down Roxboro Street where it turns into Archdale Drive and some neighbors waved me down," Scott said. They said a car had gone down an embankment

and they heard a baby crying."

Scott also heard the baby as he scrambled down a 15-foot embankment in driving rain to the car.

"The water was rising. The water level was hitting the babe's chest," Scott said. "I went through the driver's side door and pulled him

out of his seat. I pulled him to the front of the car."

Scott pulled the baby out of the car and handed him to Officer J.D. Martin who was standing on the embankment.

The child was unharmed.

• Harris, a six-year veteran of the department, was honored for resuscitating a 7-month-old girl who had stopped breathing after a traffic accident on Guess Road Oct. 24.

trunk lid and began massaging the baby's chest.

"She sort of came around. She was breathing very erratically and then she quit again," Harris said.

Harris began performing mouth-to-mouth resuscitation and the baby started to breathe. A few minutes later, the baby stopped breathing again.

"Then she came around and started crying and carrying on," Harris said.

The child, Brandy Nicole Beauparte of 2000-H Stadium Drive, was taken to Duke Hospital and held overnight for observation.

Harris visited the child and her family two weeks after the accident.

"Her father told me she didn't want to be messed with at all for two or three days after the accident, but now she's doing fine," Harris said.

"I was extremely thankful after it was all over. You just do what you have to do. I was just worried about the baby," Harris said.

Lt. R.S. Taylor, president of the Fraternal Order of Police, said the professionalism awards will be given to lodge members "every time we see the need."

The lodge includes officers from all law enforcement agencies in Durham County. About 80 percent of the police department's officers are members of the order.

"This is the lodge's way to thank you for being the officers you are," Taylor told the three officers in an awards ceremony at the Durham Police Academy on Camden Avenue.

Lodge President Reginald Taylor (left) with honorees Michael E. Harris, James L. Wood and Tony L. Scott

Durham Morning Herald/Jim Sparks

Durham baby plucked from stolen car in creek

By JANE STANCILL
Correspondent

DURHAM — Officers rushing to the scene of an accident involving a stolen car arrived early Thursday to find the vehicle half-submerged in a rain-swollen creek.

They also heard the sound of a baby crying.

In the predawn darkness, Officer T.L. Scott reached into the back seat, which was two-thirds full of cold water, and plucked the 9-month-old boy from a child safety seat.

"The water was coming up to the baby's chest, and it was still rising," Officer Scott said in an interview later Thursday. "If he had not been in the child seat, I am more than convinced he would have drowned."

The rescue ended a wild series of events during which the infant's mother had been assaulted, her car had been stolen, and the assailant had driven the car down a 15-foot embankment and smashed it into a creek — with 9-month-old Tirone D. Peace in the back.

Police described what happened this way:

About 4 a.m., Felichia M. Peace of Durham stopped at the Buy Quick Food Mart on West Corn-

> 'I just reacted when I heard the baby crying. I automatically went to the car and did what I had to do.'
>
> — Officer T.L. Scott

wallis Road to phone her father and ask him to unlock the door for her. Because it was raining heavily, she had left Tirone strapped into his infant seat in her 1980 Mercury.

As she was talking at a pay phone, a man grabbed her from behind and hung up the phone. The man — described as a slender black man with a light board — threatened her with a gun and tried to drag her in a headlock behind the store.

But Ms. Peace managed to grab a bottle from atop an ice machine and hit him in the head. She broke free and ran into the street, where she hoped to flag down a passerby.

The assailant chased her into the street and ripped off her shirt before she could get away to a nearby house, where she called police.

When Ms. Peace came outside to wait for police she saw a

terrifying sight — her car, with her son inside, was missing from the front of the store.

As police raced to the scene, they got a second call — a report of an accident on South Roxboro Street at Archdale Street, about a quarter of a mile from the store.

When officers Scott and J.D. Martin arrived, they found Ms. Peace's car half-submerged in six feet water at the bottom of a 15-foot embankment. The car apparently had skidded off the road at a sharp curve and skidded 100 feet before hitting the creek. The horn had been set off, and officers heard the sound of a baby crying. The suspect was nowhere in sight.

Officer Scott said he had little time to think. "I just reacted when I heard the baby crying," he said. "I automatically went to the car and did what I had to do."

Ms. Peace was reunited with her son as emergency medical technicians examined him on the scene. Although her car was a total loss, the baby was not hurt.

"I thought they were going to say something else when they found my baby," she said. "But they told me what I wanted to hear. Lord, I was so glad to get him back.

"They got him out just in time, thank goodness."

Officer Scott,

Thought you might like a copy of this. You're famous! This story was picked up by national wire services! Thank you for helping me tell the story.

— Jane Stancill
The News & Observer
682-4549

P.S. The mother is very grateful to you.

Uniform Patrol Bureau
Meritorious Service Award

Presented To

T. L. Scott
Officer of the Month

January 1991

This certificate is awarded as a testimony of
honest and faithful service

This 1st day of March 1991

Lt. Col. H. K. Fletcher
Operations Commander

Major C. W. Warren
Uniform Patrol Commander

Captain D. Massenburg
District One Commander

Captain R. V. Beck, II
District Two Commander

Captain J. R. Knight
District Three Commander

Captain R. W. Beck
District Four Commander

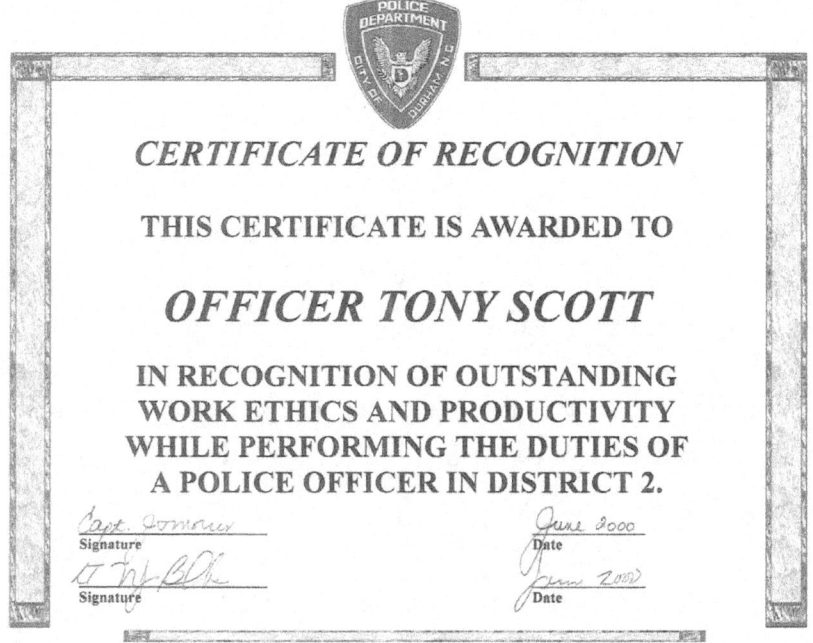

Transitioning to District 4: Maturing as an Officer

District 1 was where my foundation was laid as a rookie cop in training. It was where I began to make a name for myself and, I believe, where the nickname "Robocop" originated. My reputation for catching anyone who tried to run from me during a foot chase became well known. No one was getting away from me!

As was the practice within the Durham Police Department, once an officer completed their training in the district where they were initially assigned, they would then be reassigned to another district. For me, that next step was **District 4**, a transition that marked a new phase in my career.

It was in District 4 that I truly matured as an officer. This district gave me the opportunity to further stamp my name and build my legacy as a positive difference-maker within the community – something I took a great deal of pride in.

Building Connections in Cornwallis Projects

One of the key communities within District 4 was Cornwallis Projects. This area became a focal point of my efforts, and I made it a practice to engage directly with the people there, especially the young men.

It was nothing for me to pull up, get out of my patrol car, and talk with the youth. I would often tell them, "You've got to get it together." I didn't shy away from encouraging them to consider turning their lives around, even going as far as pointing them to Christ. This wasn't about preaching to them – it was about offering them a different perspective and reminding them that their lives had value and potential!

This approach was part of my evolution as an officer. I didn't see my role as just arresting those who needed arresting. I saw it as an opportunity to pour knowledge and wisdom into people, to encourage them to rise above their circumstances and make better choices for their futures. Furthermore, I'd learned that arresting people because I could, as required by the law or from the pressure of those who work with me, was not always necessary or the best thing to do. Every situation was different, and I took this into account!

Addressing Problems at the Root

My efforts to connect with the community didn't stop with the young people. I also spent time talking to the older residents. When responding to calls – whether for family disputes, domestic disturbances, or other issues – I took the time to figure out the root causes of the problems.

I made it my mission to address these situations thoroughly. While some of my fellow officers criticized me for spending more time than they thought necessary on certain calls, I believed in resolving issues in a way that prevented them from escalating or recurring.

This approach didn't go unnoticed. A supervisor once told me that some officers had complained about the time I spent on calls. But the supervisor's response to them was clear: "When Officer Scott goes to a call and addresses the situation, we don't have to go back. Unlike many other officers, who respond without offering a solution, Officer Scott ensures the problem is resolved."

That feedback meant a great deal to me. It validated my approach to policing and reinforced my belief that investing time in understanding and solving problems could make a lasting difference. I took great pride in knowing that my efforts were not only appreciated by my supervisors but also made a tangible impact on the community.

The Challenges and Activity in McDougald Terrace

Another significant area in District 4 was McDougald Terrace. This community presented its own set of challenges and a high level of activity. Before delving into the specific events and issues I encountered there, I want to emphasize that my approach in McDougald Terrace, as in Cornwallis Projects, was grounded in building relationships and addressing issues at their core.

The Reward of Making a Difference

As a result of being a difference-maker and striving to get to the root of problems, I've had several people approach me over the years – both during my time in law enforcement and since my retirement. They often ask, "Do you remember when such and such happened?" or "Do you remember what you said to me?"

More often than not, I don't remember the specific interactions or moments they reference. But what I do know is that hearing how something I said or did positively impacted their lives fills me with gratitude. These moments remind me that even the smallest actions or words can leave a lasting impression.

There are, however, two situations that I clearly recall. These encounters stand out because of the profound way they reflected the impact of my efforts to build relationships within the community.

The LPN

The first situation involved a man who approached me long after our initial interaction. He was a tall, imposing figure – bigger and taller than me. I remember we were in the gym when he tapped me on the shoulder, and as I turned to see who it was, I found myself face-to-face with this giant of a man.

He said, "You probably don't remember who I am." And I admitted, "I don't."

He went on to tell me that, as a young boy, he had been with his cousin when another officer (Milton Alston) and I responded to a call involving them. Apparently, someone had reported them for whatever they were doing at the time. While I didn't recall the specifics, he told me that day had stuck with him ever since.

He then shared something that truly moved me. He said, "I wanted to let you know that I became an LPN (Licensed Practical Nurse). I made it." Hearing those words and seeing the pride on his face was incredibly rewarding! To know that he had taken a positive path in life and wanted to share that with me was a powerful reminder of why I approached my work the way I did.

"You Were the Only One Who Talked to Us"

The second situation occurred while I was working an off-duty job at Burger King in District 2. I was sitting at a table, reading a book, when two men walked in. I immediately recognized them as individuals from neighborhoods I had patrolled – specifically Cornwallis Projects.

As they approached me, I admit my initial thought was, "What do they want?" But what followed was a moment that caught me completely off guard.

One of the young men said to me, "Officer Scott, I used to hate you when you came into Cornwallis Projects."

His words surprised me, but then he continued, "You were the only one who would talk to us, and I appreciate it. I wanted to let you know that I went into the armed services, I'm married, and I have a child. I've done something with my life."

Hearing that from him was deeply rewarding. Knowing that the time I spent talking to people, listening to them, and trying to guide them in the right direction had made an impression reinforced my belief in the importance of connecting with the community.

The Lasting Impact

These two encounters are just a glimpse into the many stories I've heard over the years. They remind me that the work we do as officers goes beyond enforcing the law. It's about building relationships, offering guidance, and making a difference – one person at a time.

McDougald Terrace: The Mac, A Crack Haven

McDougald Terrace, known as "The Mac," was infamous during the height of the crack cocaine epidemic sweeping through Durham. The Mac had a reputation as a hotbed for drug sales, and during my time assigned there, I saw firsthand how pervasive and destructive the drug trade was in the community.

Early in the rise of crack cocaine, the individuals selling drugs in The Mac were bold and brazen. They would stand on street corners with their drugs openly on their person, making arrests almost effortless for aggressive officers like me. I made multiple arrests during this time simply by driving up and catching them red-handed.

However, it didn't take long for their tactics to evolve. They became more strategic, hiding their drugs in various locations around the area, whether in nearby parks, bushes, or other concealed spots. Some even began relying on accomplices to hold the drugs for them, creating layers of separation between themselves and the evidence. Realizing this shift in their approach, I knew I had to adapt my strategies as well.

Creative Policing Strategies

In response to their new tactics, I began to develop my own creative methods for disrupting their operations.

It wasn't unusual for me to hide in the nearby woods, observing their activities and pinpointing where they were stashing the drugs. Once I located the hiding spots, I would seize the drugs and then make arrests. At times, I would patrol The Mac on foot in the middle of the night, dressed in camouflage attire to conceal my uniform. This allowed me to blend in with the environment and approach unnoticed. I would surprise individuals engaging in drug transactions, leading to successful arrests.

One of my more memorable strategies involved a park located within The Mac. Across from the park was a small business with a laundromat and a store. I would climb on top of the building and use it as a vantage point to watch drug transactions unfold below. After gathering enough evidence, I would climb down, track back through the woods to the opposite side of The Mac (Bacon Street), where I had parked my patrol car, and then drive back to the scene to seize the drugs and make arrests.

The individuals involved in the drug trade were often dumbfounded. They couldn't figure out how I was able to intercept their activities or where I had been watching from. My unconventional methods caught them off guard time and again, allowing me to stay one step ahead.

Building a Reputation

Through these efforts, I was able to make consistent, solid drug arrests in The Mac. My name became increasingly recognized throughout the Durham Police Department and the community as a go-getter. For me, it wasn't just about making arrests – it was about finding innovative ways to address the challenges posed by a rapidly changing drug culture.

In a place as notorious as The Mac, adapting to the environment and staying ahead of those perpetuating the drug trade was crucial. These strategies helped me disrupt illegal activities and contribute to the safety of the community, even amidst the challenges of the crack epidemic.

"10 18!!!" in The Mac

"10 18" is one of the many 10 codes that police officers must learn. When an officer says "10 18!" it alerts dispatchers and every officer on duty that the officer has something urgent to communicate. It is not a code used lightly.

In my career, I can probably count on both hands the number of times I utilized the "10 18" code. Only once did I use it because I was genuinely concerned for my personal safety. That moment occurred in McDougald Terrace.

The Warning

Earlier that day, before the situation I'm about to describe unfolded, I encountered someone I knew from my community and throughout Durham. This individual stopped me to share something he had heard on the streets. He told me that a particular drug dealer – a notorious figure who supplied the McDougald Terrace area – had been discussing having individuals from New York come to Durham to "Take me out."

The warning didn't rattle me. I responded simply: "Durham is my home. I'm not concerned. If they come, let them come." For me, it wasn't bravado but a matter of principle. This was my city, my community, and I wasn't going to let threats of violence keep me from doing my job.

The Encounter

Later that same summer afternoon, I found myself back in The Mac. I was face-to-face with the very individual who had been mentioned in the warning – the notorious drug dealer! It wasn't unusual for me to engage in conversation with people involved in illegal activities. I believed in maintaining communication, even with those on the other side of the law.

As we stood there talking, I kept the tone casual. I often said things to individuals like him, "Hey man, if you weren't selling drugs, we'd probably be friends – maybe even hanging out on this corner, having a good time. But you're doing your job, and I've got to do mine. It's the game of cat and mouse. If I catch you, I catch you. If I don't, I don't. Nothing personal. I've got a job to do."

It was a straightforward approach that often broke the tension, and I used it to maintain a level of respect, even in the midst of our opposing roles. But this particular encounter, given the warning I'd received earlier, carried an underlying weight.

A Close Call on Lakeland Avenue

I took great pride in the relationships I built within the communities I patrolled. Even with individuals engaged in illegal activities, I made it a point to foster a sense of mutual respect. I often thought – and even said aloud – that if I ever found myself in a bind, some of these individuals might come to my aid because of the rapport we had established.

But respect has its limits, especially when livelihoods are at stake. I suppose the major drug player in McDougald Terrace had grown tired of me seizing his drugs and arresting his foot soldiers. On one particular day, I found myself face-to-face with him on Lakeland Avenue, near the park and the small business I had often used as a vantage point to observe illegal activities.

As we talked, what started as a tense but manageable exchange escalated. We began to exchange what I would describe as "words." Several of the guys who worked for him were standing nearby, and I couldn't ignore how they started closing in on me!

Before I knew it, they were encircling me!

"10 18!!!" Calling for Backup

At that moment, I felt a level of tension I had never experienced before! I don't recall exactly what triggered the situation, but I knew one thing with certainty: I needed help, and I needed it fast!

Grabbing my radio, I called out: **"10 18, 10 18, I need immediate assistance!"** This was an urgency that my fellow officers had never heard from me, although I'd been in numerous intense situations.

Within moments, I could hear the sound of sirens in the distance as officers from throughout the district began responding to my call. The sound of those sirens shifted the energy of the situation. One by one, the individuals who had surrounded me began to back off and retreat.

By the time my fellow officers arrived, the tension had dissipated, and no incident occurred. For that, I am deeply grateful!

A Lesson in Vigilance

That day reinforced a critical lesson about the unpredictability of policing. No matter how much mutual respect may exist, there are moments when the stakes become too high for civility to hold.

Looking back, I'm thankful for the swift response of my fellow officers and for the instincts that led me to call for backup when I did. It was a reminder that, in this line of work, even the most experienced officer must stay vigilant because danger can arise in an instant!

God's Reminder

During this period of my life, I was growing and maturing as a Christian; God would soon remind me, "I got you, my son." This reassurance would come to mind throughout my career and beyond!

A few hours after the tense encounter with the notorious drug dealer in McDougald Terrace, I found myself reflecting on what had happened. It was late at night, and I was sitting at a secluded spot not far from The Mac, on Alston Avenue near Riddle Road. I was parked on the property then known as the Zapha Temple, taking a moment to collect my thoughts, perhaps reading as I awaited my next call. This was a common practice of mine when a shift had slowed down.

The Call

As I sat there, a call came over the radio. A co-worker – a brother ("Chuck" B.) I respected him tremendously! He was working off-duty at a local establishment where a party was taking place. He called out on his police radio: "10 18, shots fired!"

Without hesitation, I responded, heading toward the location on Fayetteville Street near Burlington Avenue!

The Crash

As I approached Highway 55, rounding the sharp corner where a Burger King now stands, I was driving a newly issued police car equipped with anti-lock braking systems (ABS). At the time, I didn't fully understand how the ABS system worked. When I entered the curve at high speed and felt the brakes pulsating, I instinctively let off the brakes – a critical mistake!

Centrifugal force took over, and I lost control of the vehicle! Unable to navigate the sharp turn, my car careened off the road and crashed into a tree! The impact was severe, and the airbag deployed with force!

God's Protection

Staggering from the wrecked vehicle (so I was told), I tried to process what had just happened. An individual who had driven up to the scene later told me, "Officer Scott, you got out of your car and then called on your radio for assistance." Looking back, I don't recall how I managed to do so. The car was *completely totaled*!

Sometime afterward, I heard a recording of the radio transmission from that night. In the recording, I heard myself calling out to dispatch, reporting that I had been in an accident and providing my location. I also mentioned seeing smoke, which I later realized was coming from the deployed airbag.

It wasn't long before EMS arrived on the scene. As they began to assess me, I remember feeling faint and telling them, "I feel myself falling faint." But before I passed out, I made one final request: "I want a praying man to ride with me in the ambulance." This was a fellow police officer and friend, Tim B, who I think rode with me. He and I would often sit in our patrol cars parked side by side. We talked about any and everything, not the least of which our faith in Jesus! My request for a god-fearing praying man and feeling faint is the only thing that I recall following the accident.

A Lesson in Faith

That night was a stark reminder of God's protection. Despite the severity of the crash, I survived with my life intact. In my moments of vulnerability, I found comfort in my faith, knowing that God was with me every step of the way, no matter what threats or any opposing forces that came at me!

A Miracle of Survival

After the crash, I was transported to Duke Emergency Hospital. By God's grace, I was released the next morning with nothing more than scratches to my legs. Reflecting on the devastation of the accident, I remember someone saying to me, "I don't know how you survived that crash."

It was nobody but God!

A Sobering Sight

In the days that followed, I went to the city compound to retrieve my personal items from the patrol car. Seeing the wrecked vehicle brought the reality of the incident into sharp focus!

I didn't recall at the time, but that night, I had been listening to gospel music on my personal radio and cassette tapes of sermons from various preachers. That memory, combined with the sight of the car's wreckage, reminded me of God's constant presence and protection.

The car was a total loss! The front end, particularly on the right side, was completely crushed! The engine had been pushed into the passenger side of the car. Had someone been sitting in the passenger seat, their fate would have been far worse than mine!

The force of the impact was so significant that it not only demolished the front of the vehicle but also caused the right windshield frame and the right side of the car's roof to buckle. Looking at the vehicle, I knew without a doubt that my survival was nothing short of a miracle!

God's Assurance

As I stood there, taking in the destruction, I felt God's voice in my heart, reminding me once again: "Son, I got you. I got you!"

God's Sustaining Hand

Through dangerous seen and unseen dangers, God clearly sustained me during my 27 years of policing in the city of Durham. As I close out this chapter, I want to highlight a few other incidents from my time in District 4. These situations, like many others I encountered, involved weapon violations. While there were numerous incidents where guns were taken off the streets as a result of my policing, here are three situations that stand out to me.

TUESDAY, AUGUST 13, 1991

THE HERALD-SUN, DURHAM, N.C.

CRASH FROM B1

the car was outfitted with an airbag, which deployed during the crash.

"The airbag saved him," the officer said.

No charges were filed Monday, but investigation was continuing.

Scott was answering a call for help about 1:35 a.m. from Sgt. N.J. Blake, who was working off-duty security at B&G Grill, to help break up a fight.

As officers responded to the call, they were told shots were being fired.

One man, Connie Clayton, 17, of 1410 Fay St., was shot in the right arm with a shotgun.

He was taken to Duke Hospital for treatment.

Scott was driving north on Old South Alston Avenue to help Blake when he lost control of the car in a curve as he approached N.C. 55 near the North Carolina Central University Law School.

The patrol car jumped a curb, crashed through a hedge and smashed into a tree.

The patrol car jumped a curb, crashed through a hedge and smashed into a tree.

Officers were unable Monday night to give an estimate of Scott's speed when the accident occurred.

Scott was able to get out of the car and call for help.

When other officers got to the B&G Grill, they found a large crowd of men and women arguing in the parking lot.

Witnesses said that after the

LOST CONTROL: Officer T.L. Scott escaped serious injury early Monday when he lost control of the car on South Alston Avenue.

The Herald-Sun/BERNHARD THOMAS

fight first broke out, one participant grabbed a shotgun and fired it at Clayton.

Bird shot from the blast damaged the rear window and trunk of Blake's personal car, which was parked nearby.

Moments later Officer R.G. Smith saw a car on Massey Avenue matching the one in which the shooting suspect left.

As Smith turned his patrol car around to stop the car, the occupants jumped out and ran.

Several spent shotgun shells were found in the abandoned car, police said.

14-Year-Old Charged With Break-In

A 14-year-old Durham boy was charged with breaking into a house on Hart Street Friday night after Durham Police Lt. J.H. Pendergrass spotted him standing near a stolen go-cart on Hart Street.

Pendergrass saw two boys standing in the street in front of Robert Bell's house at 2306 Hart St. about 9:30 p.m. When Pendergrass stopped, the boys ran. Officers chased them across

Ashe Street to Kate Street, where the 14-year-old was caught by Officer T.L. Scott. The other boy escaped.

Officers found that Bell's house had been broken into. A window was smashed out and the go-cart and a stereo system were stolen.

The 14-year-old was taken to the Durham County Youth Home on Broad Street.

Police car slams into tree, officer not seriously hurt

By KAMMIE MICHAEL
The Herald-Sun

A Durham police officer escaped serious injury early Monday when his patrol car went out of control and slammed into a tree on South Alston Avenue near N.C. 55.

The officer, T.L. Scott, was responding to an off-duty officer's request for emergency help at the B&G Grill on Fayetteville Street, where police said a fight had broken out and shots were being fired.

Scott was taken to Duke Hospital for treatment of a possible concussion and later released. Scott's patrol car, a 1991 Chevrolet Caprice, was a total loss.

"That car was totally destroyed. I've never seen a car that badly damaged where no one was killed or seriously injured," one officer said Monday.

Scott was wearing a seat belt and

See **CRASH**/B7

African American
Reading Day
at Shepard

A Gun at Fayetteville and Cook

One of these incidents occurred while I was on patrol near a local store on **Fayetteville and Cook Road**, close to Hillside High School. This area was known at the time for drug sales, particularly around the nearby car wash. As I sat in my patrol car, I struck up a conversation with a young man who stood a few feet away.

Our exchange was casual and cordial at first, but soon, I noticed something unusual! Beneath his shirt, I could see the unmistakable outline of a gun tucked into his waistband. Remaining calm, I got out of my car without letting him know that I had spotted the weapon.

As we continued talking, I slowly approached him. When the moment was right, I quickly grabbed his shirt from the outside, placing my hand directly on the gun to secure it while I put my hand on my weapon if I needed to draw it!

He began to resist, giving me some pushback. I didn't pull my weapon. However, I do remember speaking firmly: "You don't want to do this!" Thankfully, he relented without further incident. I seized the weapon and took him into custody.

The Story Behind the Gun

After the arrest, I had the chance to hear his story. He explained that he had been trying to sell the gun because his family was struggling financially. Wanting to understand more, I spoke with one of his family members, and what he told me checked out – the family was indeed facing tough times.

Situations like these are complex. On one hand, carrying a concealed weapon is a crime, especially when combined with the environment of drug activity in the area. On the other hand, this young man wasn't out to harm anyone; he was simply trying to find a way to support his family.

In a different situation, another officer might have responded more aggressively, escalating things in a way that could have ended tragically! By the grace of God, that didn't happen here.

A Justified Outcome Avoided

Looking back, I realize how close this situation came to becoming something much worse! If I had shot him, my actions likely would have been deemed justified under the circumstances. He was armed, and his initial resistance could have been interpreted as a threat!

However, I am grateful that it didn't come to that. I have never desired to take another person's life, and I am thankful that this young man, who was barely beginning to live life, is still alive today because I acted with restraint and not out of fear!

This incident is a reminder of the split-second decisions officers must make in the field and the heavy weight those decisions carry. Fear, adrenaline, or misunderstanding can sometimes lead officers to go too far. For me, I always sought to handle situations with care and restraint, knowing that every life has value and potential, no matter the circumstances.

A Changing Landscape of Respect

In the City of Durham, even as respect for law enforcement has begun to decline nationally, there has always remained a measure of respect – both during my years patrolling the city and, I believe, even now; however, sadly, it's declining. While that respect wasn't universal, it was evident in moments when individuals chose not to escalate a situation, even when they were in a position to do so.

As officers, we often encounter situations where those breaking the law could take advantage of an opportunity to harm us. Whether out of respect, restraint or some other reason, these moments didn't escalate – and for that, I credit God's grace and protection as it pertains to me, and so should you!

One of my tactics when patrolling was to drive up to a group of individuals and observe their mannerisms. I would watch for the one who became wide-eyed or flinched – a subtle tell that often revealed who might be violating the law. This method proved effective many times and led to arrests and the removal of illegal weapons and drugs from the streets.

Confiscating Weapons at McDougald Terrace

One such incident occurred in **McDougald Terrace**, specifically in the parking lot on Cooper Street. Using my tactic of driving up and observing, I approached a group of males standing near the lot. As I pulled in, the group began to slowly scatter, retreating from the area.

When I exited my vehicle and surveyed the scene, I saw two weapons lying on the ground where the men had been gathered. I quickly confiscated the firearms, taking them off the street.

Reflecting on that moment, I realized how differently it could have turned out. Those men could have chosen to draw their weapons on me as I entered the lot. They had the opportunity, and from a tactical perspective, they had the advantage. Yet, by the grace of God, they didn't take that route!

The Duffel Bag and the Sawed-Off Shotgun

Another incident took place early one Sunday morning. I noticed a young man crossing Highway 55, also known as Alston Avenue. He carried a small duffel bag, and by the way he handled it, I instinctively knew there was a long gun inside.

I intercepted him just as he exited the wooded area leading to Heartside Apartments, a neighboring community to The Mac. Confronting him without incident, I seized the bag and discovered a sawed-off shotgun along with ammunition inside.

Although the interaction itself was uneventful, what followed was one of the most frustrating moments of my career. The young man chose to file a complaint against me, claiming I had mistreated him during the encounter.

Facing Internal Affairs

That complaint led to me standing before Internal Affairs – or Professional Standards, its now called, to defend my actions. This situation was deeply disheartening. Here I was, an officer who had successfully removed a dangerous weapon from the streets without harm to anyone, yet I found myself under scrutiny based on false allegations.

This wasn't an isolated experience. Many officers face moments where their character is called into question or their actions are misrepresented.

But for me, this incident struck a particularly deep chord. It made me feel as though the years of effort, the risks I had taken, and the good I had done were for nothing.

A Turning Point

That complaint and the subsequent investigation marked a turning point in my career. It began to shift the way I viewed my role as an aggressive, proactive officer. For years, I had taken pride in policing with vigor and determination, removing weapons and drugs from the streets, and addressing crime head-on. But this incident made me question whether that approach was worth the personal cost.

I came to realize that policing is a profession where doing the right thing doesn't always shield you from criticism or false accusations. Despite the frustration, I knew I had to find a way to continue serving with integrity, even as I adjusted my approach to the job. Ultimately, what I decided to do, as most officers were already doing, was to stop being proactive and just answer my calls.

A Puzzling Arrest for Those Listening In

As a law enforcement officer, when a crime occurs in your presence or a violation of the law that's egregious, you are required to act. This principle led to a situation that, while serious at the time, became something of a funny and puzzling story among my fellow officers across the city.

The incident happened two blocks from McDougald Terrace, on Bacon St. near Lawson Avenue, near Durham Tech. As I traveled southbound on Bacon Avenue, I noticed a beverage distribution truck parked in the parking lot of the Town & Country convenience store. Two individuals were hurriedly taking beverages from the truck, clearly attempting to steal them.

Unbeknownst to them, I was coming down the hill. They never saw me. Once they grabbed the items, they split up – one running toward McDougald Terrace, the other continuing down Bacon Street towards Heartside Apts. I quickly acted! I intercepted the first suspect as he fled down Bacon Avenue, apprehending him while communicating on my police radio about the situation. With him secured, I proceeded to the parallel street, Cooper Street, where I spotted the second suspect casually walking away, likely thinking he was in the clear. Driving up to him, I made the second arrest.

This was the first time in my career that I had arrested two people in one incident, both fleeing in different directions. My ability to apprehend both suspects left my fellow officers across the city puzzled and amused as they tried to figure out how I managed it. It was a lighthearted moment in an otherwise demanding profession.

An Intense Situation on Capps Street

On a more serious note, I once responded to a call for a domestic dispute near or on Capps Street. The caller stated that their former companion refused to leave their home and was now sitting in their car.

When I arrived on the scene, I saw the individual in the car and heard the engine revving. As I approached, the situation quickly took a dangerous and unsettling turn – the car caught fire! The person inside the vehicle was unresponsive, and it became apparent to me that they may have chosen to take their own life!

The scene was intense! As flames began to engulf the vehicle, I had to consider several things at once: Was this a crime scene? Was this person's life taken from them, or was this truly a self-inflicted act? Despite the questions swirling in my mind, one thing was clear – if I didn't act, the body would be destroyed, perhaps leaving even more questions unanswered.

I made the decision to pull the individual from the car, removing them from the flames. Unfortunately, it was later determined that this person had indeed taken their own life. I had also recovered from the vehicle the firearm used.

Reflections

These two incidents – one humorous and one deeply tragic – serve as reminders of the unpredictable nature of law enforcement. In one moment, you're chasing down suspects with surprising ease, and in another, you're facing the heavy reality of life and death! Through it all, the role of an officer is to act decisively, with the hope of bringing resolution, understanding, and sometimes, even a bit of levity to the job.

A Life-Changing Encounter

Although there are many more stories to share from my uniform patrol days on the streets of Durham, I will close this chapter with perhaps the most rewarding experience of them all. This moment not only marked a high point in my career but also, in a rather unique way, helped to steer me toward a path in my spiritual maturity that I had never considered before!

The day began like many others, with roll call at the District 4 substation. My supervisor at the time was Sgt. C.R. Thompson, a good supervisor an African American man with years of experience as an officer. During roll call that morning, he made an announcement to the squad: "I need a volunteer."

Now, there's an old saying in law enforcement – never volunteer for anything because you never know what you might be signing up for. But for some reason, I decided to raise my hand that day, volunteering for the assignment. Unbeknownst to me, what awaited me would not only be thrilling but profoundly impactful!

Escorting Ms. Rosa Parks

Sgt. Thompson explained that the civil rights icon Ms. Rosa Parks was in town, staying at a hotel in District 3. My assignment was straightforward but significant: I was to meet Ms. Parks in her hotel room, escort her and her limousine driver to North Carolina Central University for her speaking engagement, and then return her safely to her hotel afterward. I met Ms. Parks in her room. I was at a loss for words! Photographer Wendy M.T. was taking pictures. I have an awesome picture with Ms. Parks that I cherish to this very day!

I carried out the assignment as instructed, meeting Ms. Parks and ensuring her journey to and from the event went smoothly. Being in her presence was surreal. As I escorted her, I couldn't help but reflect on who she was and what she represented – the courage, the strength, and the enduring legacy of her role in the civil rights movement!

A Call to Reflect

Throughout the day, I found myself replaying the experience in my mind. I thought deeply about the civil rights movement and the monumental role Ms. Rosa Parks played in helping to shape history. Her quiet defiance on that Montgomery bus was a catalyst for change, a single act of courage that reverberated through generations.

As I reflected, I felt an undeniable pull in my spirit. I found myself asking, "Okay, God, what is it that you want me to do in my life?" I can say with confidence that this book and three other books that I've published have been, in part, what **He** wanted me to do.

That question lingered in my heart long after my encounter with Ms. Parks. And it wasn't much longer after this experience that I accepted the call to preach the *Gospel – the Good News of Jesus Christ.*

Closing Thoughts

This encounter with Ms. Rosa Parks was more than just an assignment; it was a divine moment that set me on a new course. It reminded me of the power of a single act to create ripples of change and the importance of walking in faith and purpose.

As I look back on my years in uniform patrol, this experience stands out not just for its historical significance but for how it shaped my journey as a servant – not only of the people but of my God – Jehovah and the Father of His eternally existing and ***Unique*** Son, Jesus, my Lord and Savior!

CHAPTER 7

Specialized Work Assignments: C.A.T.T. & S.E.T.

It was the hot summer of 1992, and I was beginning to feel the weight of burnout from my years of service, particularly my time patrolling the streets of McDougald Terrace as an aggressive officer. Burnout is something that all officers need to recognize and address before it compromises their ability to serve effectively.

The reality of burnout is that it can lead to diminished effectiveness and even poor decision-making. For officers on the street, this can have costly consequences – for their careers, their safety, and the communities they serve. Recognizing the signs is crucial, and taking proactive steps to address them is essential. For me, it was clear that I needed a change.

Fortunately, my hard work and reputation as a go-getter didn't go unnoticed. A supervisor, recognizing my dedication and effectiveness in the field, personally sought me out for a new opportunity.

The Birth of the C.A.T. Team

At the time, the Durham Police Department was grappling with the crack epidemic that had swept through the city. To combat the rampant street-corner drug sales that were plaguing neighborhoods, the department made the decision to create a new unit: the Crime Area Target Team (C.A.T.T.).

The C.A.T. Team was a pilot initiative consisting of perhaps six to eight officers. Our mission was clear: to identify the neighborhoods most affected by drug sales, infiltrate those areas, and take meaningful action to disrupt the illegal activities taking place.

For me, being selected for this team was a turning point. It offered a chance to step away from the routine of uniform patrol and focus on a specialized assignment that promised to make a direct and tangible impact on the community.

The C.A.T.T.'s Unique Approach

As a team, our primary mission was to identify neighborhoods where street-level drug sales were rampant and causing significant harm to the community. What made our approach unique – something that set us apart from the uniform patrol officers – was the time and effort we invested in truly understanding the neighborhoods we served.

While patrol officers often didn't have the luxury of spending extended time in one area, we would immerse ourselves in the neighborhoods plagued by street-corner drug sales. We worked to establish a rapport with the residents, many of whom were fed up with the crime and chaos brought about by the drug trade.

Building Community Cooperation

More often than not, the citizens cooperated with us, willingly providing valuable information about the individuals involved in the illegal activity.

They would point out the key players – the ones responsible for bringing drugs into their neighborhoods and standing on the corners selling them. For these residents, our presence offered a glimmer of hope that something could finally be done to reclaim their streets. Their cooperation was pivotal to our success, and we were careful to treat them with the respect they deserved.

An Aggressive but Legal Approach

Once we confirmed the intelligence gathered from the community, we took a proactive and aggressive approach to address the problem. However, it was always a legal approach, operating within the boundaries of the law to ensure that our actions would hold up in court and wouldn't infringe on anyone's rights. With the information in hand, we would target the known suspects. Our operations were often swift and strategic! We'd pull up in these communities, often catching individuals off guard. We would frisk and question them, using the intel we had gathered to guide our interactions.

Sometimes, this led to immediate arrests when suspects were caught with drugs on their person. Other times, it required a more thorough canvassing of the area. We'd search for drugs or weapons stashed nearby, often in plain sight but cleverly hidden around where the suspects conducted their illegal activity.

Impacting the Streets

This method was effective not only in making arrests but also in sending a clear message: these neighborhoods were no longer safe havens for illegal activity. Our presence and actions disrupted the flow of the drug trade, creating a tangible impact that both the citizens and the suspects felt.

Community Praise and Expansion

The citizens of Durham delighted in and praised our efforts as members of the C.A.T. Team. Our proactive approach to cleaning the streets and tackling the drug trade brought a sense of relief and hope to many communities. The impact of our work was not only felt by residents but also caught the attention of the local media. The success of the pilot program was clear, and it became newsworthy across the city.

In response to our success, the Durham Police Department expanded the program the following year. A second squad was added, consisting of an additional six to eight officers. With this expansion, the C.A.T. Team was now able to provide around-the-clock coverage rather than operating solely during the day or night shifts.

There were even instances when both squads worked together, combining forces to address pressing issues or conduct large-scale operations. Things started off well, with the team's expansion promising even greater impact. However, it wasn't long before problems began to surface.

A Troubling Shift

It soon became apparent – not only to me but to a couple other officers as well – that something was amiss with the new squad. Unlike the original team, which focused on gathering intel and taking a precise, targeted approach, this second squad was adopting methods that were, at best, questionable and, at worst, outright violations of individuals' rights!

Rather than relying on intelligence or clear evidence, the new squad began indiscriminately targeting African American males standing on street corners. Their actions were based on sweeping assumptions rather than facts, treating every "Black man" in these areas as a suspect.

A Personal Conflict

As a young African American male myself, I found this deeply troubling! I understood firsthand that standing or sitting on a street corner, talking with friends, reminiscing, joking, or simply enjoying the day was a common and harmless activity. There was nothing inherently suspicious about it.

For this new squad to pull up on these individuals indiscriminately, treating them all as if they were involved in illegal activities, struck a nerve with me! Their actions weren't just poor policing – they were a violation of rights and a misrepresentation of what the C.A.T. Team was meant to be.

I wasn't alone in my concerns. As stated, a couple of other officers (W.F. and D.B.) on the C.A.T. Team began to also take notice. The very integrity of the program was at stake, and for me, it became increasingly difficult to reconcile what I saw happening with the purpose we had set out to achieve. I'll come back to these other officers shortly.

A Turning Point

When the second squad was added to the C.A.T. Team, we initially worked well together. Both squads accomplished great things throughout the community, and we were proud of the impact we were making. The collaborative efforts between the squads led to meaningful progress in reducing street-level drug activity, and for a time, it felt like the expansion of the program was a resounding success.

However, as time went on, as stated, I began to notice questionable activity emerging within the second squad. Their methods, which started to blur the line between proactive policing and rights violations, began to tarnish the reputation of the entire team, as far as I saw things. This behavior didn't affect everyone in either squad, but its influence seeped into both squads, creating a dynamic that made me increasingly uneasy.

Distancing Myself

As the questionable – and at times outright illegal – practices of certain team members became more apparent, I made a conscious decision to distance myself. I could no longer align with actions that went against the principles of fair and lawful policing.

Rather than engaging in their activities, I began to operate independently, much like I had during my time in District 4. I returned to the tactics I had relied on before, focusing on precision and legality and ensuring that my work adhered to the values I held as an officer.

Policing in West Durham

One memorable example of my approach during this period occurred in the West Durham community (Morehead Ave. area). This area had a large cemetery that stretched for blocks, offering a vantage point that allowed me to observe a nearby street where a great deal of street-corner drug activity was taking place.

Using the cemetery as cover, I would approach from the backside, dressed in camouflage clothing to remain unseen. With binoculars in hand, I would lie in position and observe the activities unfolding. Much like I had done in District 4, I used this time to carefully identify the players and pinpoint where the drugs were being stashed.

Once I had gathered sufficient evidence, I would act, seizing the drugs and making arrests. This method was deliberate and focused, ensuring that I targeted those directly involved in illegal activities while upholding the principles of lawful policing.

Staying True to My Values

The work I did during this time was a direct response to the troubling behavior I observed within the expanded C.A.T. Team. While I remained committed to addressing the drug epidemic in Durham, I felt it was essential to distance myself from any practices that violated the rights of the people we were sworn to serve.

By returning to the tactics and methods I knew to be effective and ethical, I was able to continue making an impact while staying true to my values. It was a challenging time, but it reminded me of the importance of integrity and the responsibility that comes with wearing the badge.

The Challenge of Working Alone

As I began to work alone, chatter amongst my squad members started to grow. They noticed my decision to distance myself from the group, and it didn't go without questions being raised. While there's no official "code of silence" in law enforcement, there was at this time in my career an unspoken expectation of loyalty and group cohesion – especially in specialized units like the C.A.T. Team. Officers are expected to stick together, to have each other's backs no matter the situation. While this loyalty can serve as a strength, it can also be dangerous when it enables questionable or outright bad behavior to go unchecked!

My decision to distance myself, while rooted in my commitment to ethical policing, was seen as a break from this unspoken loyalty. As I continued to work independently, two incidents occurred that made me question whether my commitment to the group was being deliberately tested – or whether my peers had begun to view me with suspicion for not following their lead.

The Struggle and the Supervisor

One incident, in particular, stood out to me. I was conducting a traffic stop, and as I seem to recall, the suspect fled the vehicle after pulling over. I immediately gave chase, catching up to him not long after. A struggle ensued as I worked to restrain and handcuff him!

During the tussle, a sergeant arrived on the scene. I remember seeing him pull up, and I expected that he would step in to assist me, as any supervisor would in such a situation. But to my surprise, he didn't! The struggle went on for what felt like an extended period of time – long enough for him to have intervened. Despite his inaction, I was able to successfully subdue and arrest the individual without harm to either of us.

After the situation was under control, I approached my sergeant and looked at him as if to ask why he hadn't stepped in. His response was, "I couldn't get my seatbelt loose."

I remember staring at him, questioning his sincerity. Was this an excuse? Was he afraid? Or was this his way of sending a message to me about my decision to distance myself from the group? I didn't have an answer then, and I still don't know for certain what his reasoning was. But the incident left me unsettled. As best as I can recall, sometime later, this person was forced to leave DPD; it had to do with his "truthfulness," so I was told.

Reflections on Loyalty and Integrity

This moment underscored the tension I was beginning to feel within the team. While I was getting the job done and continuing to contribute to the mission of the C.A.T. Team, my decision to step away from certain group dynamics was clearly creating friction.

Loyalty in law enforcement can be a double-edged sword. On one hand, it fosters trust and cooperation among officers, which is vital in dangerous situations. But when loyalty becomes blind allegiance – when it allows questionable behavior to go unchecked – it can compromise the integrity of the unit and the profession as a whole.

For me, distancing myself was a matter of principle. I couldn't condone or participate in practices that went against the values I believed in, even if it meant facing subtle or overt pushback from my peers.

Questioning My Commitment

The second incident involving a fellow squad member on the C.A.T. Team stands out in my memory as a moment of both reflection and testing. Looking back now, it seems as though this was a strategic effort by my superiors or others to gauge exactly where my mind was when it came to policing with this unit.

By this time, I had accepted the call to preach the *Gospel of Christ*. My conscience was clear, and my convictions about right and wrong – what was ethical and what wasn't – were firmly rooted in both my faith and the teachings of the Bible. I believed in living by these principles, even as I carried out my duties as a police officer… there being no contradiction.

That being said, I also clearly recognized that those in positions of authority – whether in law enforcement or other like fields – hold roles ordained by God. Because of this, I understood that I had not only the right but also the responsibility to carry out my job effectively, even if it meant making difficult decisions, such as taking someone's life to protect others or myself. The challenge wasn't doing the job – it was ensuring that I did it ethically, lawfully, and in line with my conscience.

A Questionable Plan

This incident took place during a shift with another officer from the C.A.T. Team. We were patrolling together when we came upon a stolen vehicle on a very tight street. I was in the passenger seat, and the other officer was driving.

As we approached the vehicle, he proposed a course of action that I immediately recognized as both dangerous and tactically unsound. His plan was to pull our patrol car up directly beside the stolen vehicle to box it in, which would have exposed me – the passenger – directly to the driver of the stolen car.

This decision wasn't just reckless; it also went against police training. It was neither tactical nor safe, and I knew it was an unnecessary risk to my life. I insisted, "You are not going to pull up beside this car!"

The car wasn't stopped, and because of my refusal to allow his plan, the stolen vehicle was able to get away. As far as I was concerned, avoiding a dangerous and poorly conceived maneuver was the right decision. Due to the inherent dangers of police car chases, nationally, many police agencies began making strict policies regarding vehicle pursuits… DPD was one such agency.

Probing Questions

What followed was interesting. The officer began to probe me with various questions about the incident, and I couldn't help but feel that these questions were less about curiosity and more about assessing where I stood. It seemed he was trying to gauge my commitment – whether to the group or to the methods that had become commonplace among some members of the C.A.T. Team.

For me, my decision was simple: I refused to compromise my safety or my principles for the sake of a questionable tactic. I believed then, as I do now, that doing the job properly means doing it ethically and by the book. No badge or uniform gives anyone the right to violate those standards, and I wasn't going to bend, even if it meant drawing scrutiny from my peers or superiors.

Staying True to Myself

This incident further solidified my approach to policing. While I respected the authority of my superiors and the responsibilities of the role,

I was unwavering in my belief that every action had to align with the law, ethics, and my conscience. Even so, everyone didn't need to go to jail or have multiple charges heaped up on them. Or their car towed and impounded when it could be parked safely with the consent of the driver. These practices were common within the C.A.T.T. Team by most officers.

My faith and my calling as a preacher only strengthened this resolve. I understood that my duty to serve and protect included serving and protecting the integrity of the profession itself. For me, this meant standing firm, even when it wasn't popular or easy!

A Question of Conviction

The coworker I was patrolling with that day regarding the stolen car was someone I had known for years and genuinely liked. He had a personality larger than life – stubborn, outspoken, and not one to shy away from sharing his opinion. While I valued our working relationship, I also understood his character well enough to know how to deal with him.

During our patrol, and following the stolen car getting away, he asked me a direct and pointed question: "Can you shoot a man in the line of duty and kill him?" It was a question that carried weight, especially given the nature of our work and the growing tensions within the squad. But knowing his bullheaded personality, nevertheless, I chose to respond evasively.

My response was simple yet deliberate: "The Bible says, thou shall not kill."

That was all I said.

My True Beliefs

While my response to him was intentionally brief, my true beliefs on the matter were much deeper. As a police officer, I understood the gravity of the role I held. According to state and federal law, I was authorized to use deadly force when necessary to protect others or myself.

But my understanding went beyond the law of the land. My faith and my study of the Bible, particularly the New Testament, affirmed that God has ordained those in positions of authority to rule and protect the land. As *Romans 13:4* states, ***"They do not bear the sword for nothing."***

This meant that if I had to take a life in the line of duty, I would be justified not only by the law of the land but also in the eyes of God. I knew this, and I was prepared to act accordingly if the situation ever required it. However, I also believe that deadly force should be a last resort, used only when absolutely necessary!

Voices of Concern

Shortly after this exchange, I had an encounter with two other officers (B/Ms) who were also questioning the practices of the new squad members. These officers, like me, had begun to notice the ways in which some members of the C.A.T. Team were violating people's rights!

I found them standing together in one of the local projects (Dearborn) in the Bragtown area, deep in discussion. As I approached, it quickly became clear what they were talking about. They expressed their concerns openly, acknowledging the troubling shift in how some of our colleagues were conducting themselves.

As they spoke, I listened, but I also realized that talk alone wouldn't change anything. Someone needed to address the matter directly. Finally, I said, "I am going to say something to our supervisor." They stood silent.

Taking a Stand

As far as I know, I was the only one who stepped up to address the issue. Speaking out was not an easy decision, especially in a profession where loyalty to the group is often prioritized over calling out wrongdoing. But my conscience wouldn't allow me to stay silent.

I knew there would be consequences for speaking up, and I accepted that. However, I did not expect what would occur! Taking a stand against questionable practices was not just a matter of ethics – it was a matter of integrity. It was about upholding the oath I had taken and staying true to the values that guided me both as an officer and as a man of faith.

The Aftermath

While I'll share more about the consequences of this decision momentarily, this moment marked a turning point. It was a test of my commitment to doing what was right, even when it was difficult. And though it came at a cost, I have no regrets about standing up for what I believed in.

Reflections on the Streets and a Fallen Friend

Just as I shared only a fraction of my experiences patrolling the streets in District 4 and beyond, there are a number of stories I could tell about my time as a C.A.T.T. officer. The work we did revealed the devastating grip that drugs, particularly crack cocaine, had on our city and its communities.

However, rather than recounting numerous tales, I will share one story that not only sheds light on how drugs affected Durham but also honors the memory of a coworker I greatly respected and admired: Milton Alston, a classmate of mine while going through the academy.

A Dedicated Partnership

Milton and I worked closely together during the height of the crack epidemic. He was more than just a coworker; he was a dedicated and principled officer, someone you could count on in the field – and a friend. It was actually Milton who was with me during the incident involving the two little boys, one of whom later became an LPN and thanked me for the impact I had on his life.

Milton and I shared a mutual concern for the Pilot Street housing complex (410 Pilot St, if my memory is correct), a dilapidated and run-down building that had become a hub for illegal activity in District 4. The building may have housed anywhere from 50 to 100 individuals, many living in deplorable conditions. If you've ever seen the movie **New Jack City**, this complex could easily have been attached to the project unit depicted in that film.

The complex was notorious for drug sales, drug usage, the distribution of stolen items, and other criminal activities. It was a place that demanded attention, and Milton and I were committed to addressing the problems there. However, this was easier said than done. The building was secure; therefore, the arrival of the police would not go unnoticed – hence easier said than done.

Entering the Complex

I remember one night in particular when Milton and I decided to investigate the building further. Gaining access was no easy task. Utilizing the element of surprise, I climbed into a vacant room through an opening to where an air conditioning unit once was. Once I gained access, I opened the door for Milton to enter. To enter this building, one had to be let in, or a key card was used to gain entrance.

What we found inside was a reflection of what we had observed from the outside – chaos, squalor, and the devastating effects of a community engulfed in crime and addiction. While the specific details of that night have faded over time, I am certain we made arrests and took steps to disrupt the illegal activity taking place there.

Honoring Milton Alston

Milton Alston was not only a hardworking and dedicated officer but also a man of integrity with a big heart. And he could be a clown, aka funny! He later transitioned to become a federal agent, continuing his service in law enforcement. However, his career and life ended under tragic and, to some, me included, mysterious circumstances.

The story of Milton's death has been told in at least two ways. One version claims that he took a person's life, and he then took his own life, but I do not believe this to be true! I knew the man personally! Milton was a man of principle who, like me, stood his ground for what was right. I believe his unwavering commitment to integrity cost him his life in the corrupt city where he had been assigned, New Orleans.

As far as I am concerned, along with others who knew him as a friend, while the exact details of his passing may never be fully known, we question the narrative provided. What I do know is this: Milton Alston was a man who stood for justice and what was right from wrong, who worked tirelessly to make a difference, and who lived with integrity. His legacy is one of courage and dedication!

Closing Thoughts

The work Milton and I did on Pilot Street and throughout Durham was a testament to our shared commitment to confronting the challenges of the crack epidemic head-on. While the task was daunting and often heartbreaking, it was officers like Milton who made it possible to persevere.

This story and his memory remind me of the importance of maintaining integrity in the face of adversity and staying true to the principles that guide us, both as officers and as human beings.

Taking a Stand II

Taking a stand against wrongdoing is challenging enough, but it becomes even more difficult when you know there may be consequences for doing so. For me, the choice was clear. My conscience, grounded in my faith and commitment to ethical policing, convicted me to act.

I decided to confront the issues I had observed within the C.A.T. Team. The addition of the second squad had created dynamics that I believed were undermining the integrity of the unit and the trust we had worked so hard to build with the community. Questionable practices were becoming more common, and it was clear to me that these actions needed to be addressed.

Confronting My Supervisor

The first step I took was to bring my concerns to my immediate supervisor – the same individual who had handpicked me to be on the team. I shared my observations about the other squad and how their behavior was negatively affecting the unit as a whole. I told him plainly, "Something needs to be said; what they are doing is not right."

His reaction was one of shock and offense, as if he were thinking, "Who do you think you are? How dare you approach me?" It was clear that my comments had caught him off guard.

Shortly afterward, during our assembly, he addressed the squad, offering some remarks about policing. But his comments were surface-level generic and didn't address the root of the issues I had raised. I couldn't let it go.

Afterward, I looked at him and said, "That wasn't enough."

Those three words set something in motion. From that moment on, I believe my supervisor began considering how he could remove me from the squad. Looking back, it's clear to me that my actions that day planted a seed of tension between us, one that would grow in the days and weeks to come.

Going Over His Head

As the situation within the squad failed to improve, I knew I needed to escalate my concerns. This was not just a matter of internal disagreements

– it was about upholding the values of justice and accountability that the department and our profession were supposed to stand for.

I decided to go over my supervisor's head and speak directly with the command staff. I met with a member of the command staff and shared my concerns about what I was seeing within the C.A.T. Team. After I finished speaking, I sat quietly, listening to their response. The individual acknowledged the seriousness of the issue, saying something along the lines of, "If this is the case, this could cause problems for the Durham Police Department."

They went on to explain some of the potential consequences, including the possibility of a citizen review board being brought in to investigate DPD, the involvement of federal agencies, and even the loss of accreditation for the department. It was clear that they saw the issue as a legitimate concern. However, after our conversation, I never spoke with this person – or with my immediate supervisor – about the matter again.

Reflections

As I look back on this moment, I realize how pivotal it was. By speaking out, I placed myself in a vulnerable position within the department. I had challenged the status quo and disrupted the unwritten code of loyalty that often governs units like the C.A.T. Team. My actions set a series of events in motion that would ultimately have consequences for me, both professionally and personally! But even now, I stand by the decision I made. Integrity and accountability are not negotiable, and the responsibility to uphold them sometimes comes at a cost.

The Fallout

I don't know if my supervisor had begun to take the matter personally after I spoke up or if the command staff had said anything to him about my concerns. But looking back, it became clear to me that he had it in for me.

My reputation as a hardworking and reliable officer preceded me. Everyone knew that I was dedicated to the job and worked hard to make a difference. Because of this, I believe my supervisor knew that if he wanted to remove me from the squad, he would have to find something tangible – something he could use against me. And, unfortunately, for me, he did.

An Off-Duty Incident

At the time, I was working an off-duty assignment at a nightclub. It was a typical night until someone tried to enter the club with a small baggie of marijuana. Officers are often faced with situations like this, and discretion is a tool we frequently use to handle minor offenses. In this case, I made a judgment call.

Rather than arresting the individual or turning the marijuana into evidence, I chose a different approach. I escorted him to the restroom, had him dispose of the marijuana in the toilet, and watched as he flushed it away. Afterward, I denied him entry into the club for the night and sent him on his way.

It wasn't an unusual decision; discretion is a part of policing, and officers use it for a variety of reasons depending on the situation. To me, this felt like a minor incident, nothing worth reporting or dwelling on.

The Suspension

A few days later, I returned to work with the C.A.T. Team, expecting it to be a normal day. However, as I entered the office, I was met by my immediate supervisor. He handed me an envelope containing a letter that would shake me to my core. I still have this letter filed away.

The letter stated that I had been **suspended with paid leave pending an investigation**. It alleged that I had violated the police department's policies regarding the destruction of evidence, the failure to properly turn in evidence, and possibly one or two other violations that I can't recall now.

Then came the final blow: ***"I need you to hand me your badge. And/or I could not work off-duty).***

I was allowed to keep my weapon, but I was effectively sidelined and sent home to await the outcome of the investigation.

A Heavy Burden

The weight of that moment was immense. I was a young husband with two young children at home, and suddenly, my livelihood – the security and stability of my family – was in jeopardy!

I was shook to my core! I hadn't expected this. The decision I had made at the nightclub seemed so minor at the time, a routine exercise of discretion. But now, it had been turned into something much larger, something that threatened my career and reputation. How my decision on that night at the club got back to my supervisor… I can only speculate.

As I left the office that day, the uncertainty of what lay ahead consumed me for all of a day! Then a peace came over me that was from none other than my God. Nothing else about this unusual peace can make rational sense.

Reflections

This moment was a direct consequence of taking a stand! While I'll never know for certain what motivated my supervisor's actions, the timing and circumstances made it hard to ignore the connection. Still, even in the midst of fear and uncertainty, I held onto my belief that integrity and doing what was right were non-negotiable!

A Moment at the Altar

Before moving forward with my story, there's a moment I must revisit – a pivotal experience that happened before I approached my supervisor about the troubling practices within the C.AT. Team.

It was during an **altar call** at church, a time of prayer and reflection. As I stood among the congregation, I felt the weight of what I was about to do. Confronting the issues within the Durham Police Department, and specifically within the C.A.T. Team, wasn't something I took lightly. I knew it would take courage, and I knew it could lead to consequences!

In that moment of prayer, I spoke openly, asking the congregation to join me in lifting up our city's new chief of police. I remember saying, "Let's pray for the new chief of police. He has a hard job to do."

Then, I added a personal request: "Pray for me as I'm about to address the issues that I see within the Durham Police Department that are not right." I didn't go into specifics or share any details, but my tone reflected the seriousness of what I was about to undertake.

The Church Connection

Unbeknownst to me at the time, there was an individual in the congregation and maybe one other person who had a close or working relationship with my supervisor. It wasn't until later, after reflecting on everything that unfolded, that I began to wonder: Did my prayer request make its way back to my supervisor? Had this church member (s) who I'd worked closely with on the S.E.T. Team and within the church say something to my supervisor and his friend... I'm certain that he did. However, it's merely my speculation. Maybe it was the other person.

It seems plausible, even likely, that my words were shared with him. If that was the case, it could explain why my supervisor's reaction to my concerns felt so personal, almost as if he had been preparing for my challenge before I initially brought my concerns before him.

Reflections

Looking back, that moment of prayer was significant for more reasons than one. On a spiritual level, it reaffirmed my reliance on God for guidance and strength as I prepared to confront the issues I saw. But on a practical level, it set the events that followed and that which has been stated in motion.

Whether my prayer request did, in fact, reach my supervisor or not, I know this: speaking up was the right thing to do, even though it came with risks. And in that moment at the altar, I found the resolve to face those risks, trusting that God would see me through.

A Peace Beyond Understanding

The shock of being suspended from duty hit me hard at first! My badge was taken, and my livelihood was suddenly in jeopardy! As a young husband and father with two small children at home, the weight of that uncertainty was overwhelming!

But something remarkable happened about 24 hours later. A profound sense of peace washed over me – a peace that I can only attribute to God comforting me in my time of distress. It was as if He was reminding me that He was in control, even in this trying situation. Additionally, I reached out to my pastor. I shared my situation with him. Without delay, he wrote a letter to the *Chief of Police* – who, by the way, was a Deacon at his church. For my Pastor's letter, I remain grateful!

For the next three months or so, while I remained on paid suspension, I began to feel like I was on an unexpected vacation. Though I didn't have the clarity I wanted about what lay ahead, I was able to rest in the assurance that God had a plan.

Seeking Answers

Despite the initial peace, I couldn't ignore the uncertainty surrounding the investigation. No one from the Durham Police Department had reached out to me during this time, leaving me in the dark about the status of the investigation against me. After about three months of silence, I decided to take matters into my own hands. I called the department to inquire about the investigation and was directed to speak with ***Detective A.J. Carter.***

The Conversation with Detective Carter

Detective Carter was someone I knew and respected, though I hadn't had much personal interaction with him before this moment. He was known as a fine officer and a man of integrity. Later in life, he also became a licensed minister of the gospel of Jesus Christ, a calling that reflected his deep commitment to serving others. Sadly, he passed away about 10 years ago, leaving this earth far too soon. He was someone that I later called a friend and brother in Christ.

When I spoke with him, I could sense his sincerity and honesty. He didn't sugarcoat the situation but spoke to me candidly.

"Scott," he said, "I'm going to be honest with you. Let me tell you what they are saying about you."

Then he began to outline the accusations that had been circulating:

- "With your newfound religion, you've become a loner."
- "You're planning on having federal agencies come in to investigate the Durham Police Department."
- "You're unable to shoot a person in the line of duty."
- And perhaps the most significant one: "You're possibly suicidal."

I was stunned! These accusations didn't just paint a false picture of me; they were deeply personal and damaging. It was clear that someone, or perhaps multiple people, were determined to ruin my career and discredit me as an officer.

Reflections on the Accusations

Hearing these allegations confirmed what I had suspected: there was a deliberate effort to push me out of the department. The accusations were baseless, yet they spoke volumes about how far some were willing to go to undermine me.

- **A "loner" because of my faith?** My decision to distance myself from unethical practices wasn't about isolation; it was about integrity.

- **Federal investigation?** While I had raised concerns about C.A.T.T's questionable actions, my intent was always to improve the department, not to tear it down. This matter did not even originate with me but rather with the Major that I'd spoken to.

- **Inability to shoot?** This accusation struck at the heart of my professionalism, ignoring my understanding of both the legal and moral justification for using deadly force when necessary.

- **Possibly suicidal?** This was perhaps the most hurtful and outrageous claim, suggesting not only that I was unfit for duty but also attacking my character and mental health!

It was clear to me that these allegations weren't about truth; they were about creating a narrative to justify removing me from the department!

Moving Forward

While this conversation confirmed that someone, or multiple people, were out to destroy my career, it also strengthened my resolve. I knew I had done nothing wrong, and I was determined to stand firm in my faith and my principles, no matter what came next.

Detective Carter's honesty was a gift, even if the information he shared was difficult to hear. It reminded me that in every challenge, there are people who value integrity and truth. And though I didn't know how this situation would resolve, I trusted that God would see me through, just as He always had.

After my conversation with Detective A.J. Carter, I found myself ushered yet again before Internal Affairs. This time, the focus of the sergeant in charge, the same sergeant regarding the person I'd arrested with the shotgun – this sergeant being a person whose home I'd visited, whose daughter was interested in me and a family I'd taken a day trip with – questioning caught me completely off guard; I'm not sure, this person may have also been at the church on this particular Sunday… If not, perhaps an infrequent member of the church. He specifically questioned me about the ***prayer request*** I had made during service, the one where I asked for prayers for the new chief of police and for myself as I prepared to address the issues I saw within the department.

The recorder was turned on by the investigator in Internal Affairs, I was told that my prayer request had discredited the police department and that I should never make such a request again.

I opposed this accusation immediately. ***"As a Christian,"*** I stated, ***"I have the right to make any kind of prayer request that I choose to make. And***

that I was not seeking to discredit DPD." That was my stance, and I stood firmly on it!

Apart from this confrontation, I don't recall much else from that interview. But that particular moment stuck with me. It was disheartening to see my faith, something that gave me strength and clarity, being twisted into a weapon against me.

Meeting the Staff Psychologist

Shortly after the Internal Affairs interview, I was informed that I would need to meet with the ***staff psychologist*** before I could be cleared to return to duty. This was yet another step in what felt like a never-ending process, but I welcomed the opportunity to speak with this individual.

The psychologist instructed me to take an evaluation, a test designed to assess my mental stability. I completed the test and awaited the follow-up meeting to discuss the results.

When I returned for the follow-up, the conversation went along these lines:

- The psychologist began, "It seems to me that you need people to affirm you."
- I responded honestly, "Yeah, there was a time when that was something I needed, but that's not something I need now."

Then he made another observation: "You are quite truthful. The test shows that you are indeed a truthful individual."

He concluded, "I see no reason why you shouldn't be able to return to work."

Returning to Uniform Patrol

Shortly afterward, I was cleared to return to duty. However, I was no longer assigned to the C.A.T. Team. Instead, I was reassigned to uniform patrol. While this reassignment may have seemed like a step back to some, I saw it as an opportunity to refocus and continue serving the community in a way that aligned with my values. My time with the C.A.T. Team had been marked by challenges, both external and internal, but I came away from the experience with a clearer sense of who I was and what I stood for.

Reflections

This chapter of my career was one of the most trying periods of my life! From being questioned about my faith to undergoing evaluations to prove my fitness for duty, the process was quite interesting, to say the least. Yet through it all, I held onto my convictions and trusted that God had a purpose in it all.

Returning to uniform patrol was a fresh start, and though it wasn't the path I had anticipated, it allowed me to continue serving with integrity and to focus on making a positive impact in the community I cared so deeply about.

Reflections on a Cloud

The events surrounding the C.A.T. Team happened more than 30 years ago, but the weight of that time followed me throughout my career. It felt like a cloud – a lingering presence that hovered above me as I interacted with fellow officers over the years. While it didn't hinder my progress or ability to do my job, the memory of that experience and the dynamics of those days stayed with me.

Now, having been retired for 10 years, I've had time to reflect on my career and the lessons I've learned. Interestingly, in this time of retirement, I've had three conversations that directly pointed back to my time with the C.A.T. Team. These conversations have brought clarity, closure, and even a sense of validation about what I went through.

I've received permission to share the stories of two of the individuals I spoke with, and I will recount them in the order in which they occurred.

Gerald Allen: The Streets Knew

The first conversation was with Gerald Allen, someone I first met during my time as a C.A.T.T. member. When we first crossed paths, Gerald had his struggles with drugs and life on the streets. But when I reconnected with him later, his life had completely turned around – he to was a Christian! He was doing well for himself, and our conversation reflected the growth he had experienced.

Gerald shared something that both amused and surprised me. He recalled the days when he and others on the street would ask each other, "Who's on duty?" More specifically, "Which C.A.T.T. officer is working?"

He laughed as he recounted how the mood would shift when the answer came back: "Scott's working." According to Gerald, if they heard I was on duty, they'd all "pack up for the day" because they knew challenges were ahead.

While his recollection brought laughter and a smile to my face, it was what he said next that truly caught me off guard. He went on to say that back in those days, he and the guys on the street knew that the C.A.T. Team had it in for me. "They were trying to take your job," he told me.

Hearing this left me blown away! To know that even those on the street were aware of the internal dynamics and tensions within the team was shocking! This also confirmed what I had long suspected: that there were individuals who had been actively working against me during my time on the C.A.T. Team.

Sergeant Ryan Wiggins: A Chilling Parallel

The second conversation was with Sergeant Ron Wiggins (W/M), a retired former officer with the Durham Police Department. Ron and I had crossed paths again in retirement when I saw him working at the Harley-Davidson dealership near my home. Both of us were Harley riders, and we struck up a conversation about our shared experiences in law enforcement. We also discussed riding together.

As we reminisced, I opened up about what I went through during my time on the CAT team. To my utter surprise, Ron revealed that he had also been a member of the C.A.T. Team – after my departure. He listened intently as I described the challenges I faced, and then he said something that astonished me! He said, ***"Man, what you're saying to me is giving me chills. They tried to do the same thing to me!"***

According to Ron, many – if not all of the same people who were on the C.A.T. Team during my time were still there when he joined. And just as they had done with me, they tried to undermine him and create issues for him as well.

Hearing Ron's account confirmed that what I experienced wasn't isolated or unique. It was a pattern of behavior that extended beyond my time with the team, and it underscored the toxic dynamics that had plagued the unit. It's not necessary to attempt to recall all that Ron shared with me. However, I will share this comment he made. He said, "After my experience, I found it difficult to trust any officer." Sadly, the matter of trust with him after his experience extended beyond police officers, he further indicated. I clearly understood where he was coming from... I got it; I was in a similar boat! Unfortunately, Ron and I did not get to ride together; a few weeks later, he transitioned while in his sleep. Ron was truly a good person who would speak the truth, calling things as they were.

Reflections in Retirement

These conversations, while surprising, have been deeply validating. They reminded me that the struggles I faced were evil intended, and they left an impression on others, both inside and outside the department.

Gerald Allen's perspective from the streets and Ron Wiggins' account from within the team revealed the same truth: there were forces working against me during my time on the C.A.T. Team! While I've made peace with that chapter of my life, these stories serve as a powerful reminder of the challenges I faced and the integrity I maintained through it all!

Even now, decades later, I remain grateful for the lessons learned and the people who have shared their perspectives with me, bringing clarity and closure to a pivotal period in my career. As for the supervisor who was over the C.A.T. Team, who hand-picked me and who I addressed with the team's problems. Let me say this first before he targeted me... I sincerely like this person. I've described him as being quite smart and intelligent, a person who I respected and held in high regard. Nevertheless, I think his attributes and pride ultimately worked against him. I don't recall the details. However, he began to butt heads with the Chief of police (who my former pastor had written a letter to stating my character and work in the church), and this *power play* between my former supervisor and the Chief became quite public. Overseeing C.A.T.T. as a supervisor, if I recall correctly, this would be the last job he had with DPD.

Prelude: The C.A.T. Team - Next, the S.E.T. Team Experience

Just before I joined the C.A.T. Team, I had completed two weeks of training to become a member of the **Selective Enforcement Tactical Team (S.E.T.T.)**. Known for its high-risk and specialized assignments, S.E.T.T. is seen as an elite unit within the department. I was eager to expand my skills and contribute to the department in new ways.

Recently, during my retirement, I had an eye-opening conversation with Sgt. Robert Moore, another retired officer and someone I consider a friend. Within the past couple of years, Robert shared something with me that shed light on the challenges I faced – not just on the C.A.T. Team but even before that, during my time with S.E.T.T.

A Familiar Pattern

Robert explained that, much like on the C.A.T. Team, there were individuals on S.E.T.T. who didn't care for me and didn't want me to join their ranks. He mentioned one officer by name, someone who had openly voiced opposition to me becoming a part of the team.

According to Robert, this officer's reasoning had little to do with my abilities or qualifications and everything to do with my faith and my resolve to do things the right way. He told Robert, "Well, he likes to be by himself. He likes to read his Bible," and other dismissive remarks meant to discredit me.

Standing Up

While some sought to exclude me, Robert stood up for me. He pushed back against their criticisms, telling them, "Hey, he's his own man." Robert, much like I was, was someone who valued integrity and professionalism and being his "own man." He didn't shy away from speaking his mind, and he wasn't afraid to challenge the status quo. However, as best as I know, he didn't encounter the same level of resistance that I did... besides, he was a supervisor (Cpl.). Perhaps it was because of my overt expression of faith, or perhaps it was because I wasn't willing to compromise my principles to fit in that I received major pushback.

Looking Ahead

This revelation from Robert confirmed what I had long suspected: my refusal to conform to certain behaviors and practices made me a target, not just on the C.A.T. Team but even earlier, during my time with S.E.T.T.

Though I ultimately completed the training and earned my place, the experience highlighted the challenges of standing firm in one's beliefs in environments where group loyalty and conformity often take precedence.

More will be said about my time on the S.E.T. Team in the next chapter as I reflect on the lessons learned and the experiences that shaped my career.

North Carolina Highway Patrol

TONY L. SCOTT

Having Satisfactorily Completed

FUNDAMENTALS OF EXECUTIVE PROTECTION

Is Awarded This Certificate This _12th_ Day of _July_ , One Thousand Nine Hundred and _Ninety-One_ .

CAT officers on anti-drug patrol

Jerry Johnson, from left, Tony Scott and John Dermott do their duties on foot on Rosedale Avenue

Staff photo by Rob Cross

Police frustrate drug dealers' deals

By JANE STANCILL
Staff writer

Neighborhoods get CAT help

DURHAM — Eric Price moved his family from New York City to Durham last year to get away from drugs and crime.

The father of four, he settled into a house on Cobb Street in the Lyon Park area. He felt safe.

Then he noticed traffic going in and out of another house on his block. Lots of traffic. At all hours of the day.

"There's no place to go in this country to avoid this," he said. "There's no place to run."

But for now, at least, Price and his neighbors are getting some help. It started in October, when the Durham Police Department's new Crime Area Target Team descended on the area.

The 11-member squad was formed after the city council approved money to hire the

year — 28.

The CAT team spent its first six weeks in the troubled West End area, along with the adjacent neighborhoods of Lyon Park and Burch Avenue. Residents there have been overrun by crack dealers and the crime that follows a bustling drug trade.

Break-ins and robberies have increased. Neighbors say it isn't

Residents say young men stand in the streets all hours of the day, stopping cars, presumably to solicit drug business.

Police chose West End as their first target for one main reason: Residents had become so frustrated they had already banded together. And they say that organization is the key to success.

"They have a strong community," said Lt. Paul J. Martin, leader of the team. "The people have been very supportive, and

CAT helps in Durham drug war

Continued from page 1B

want to go in and alienate anyone. We're there to help."

The squad's philosophy is different from that of most patrols. Instead of responding to crimes, they try to prevent them.

Since the beginning, Martin and other team members have been to 12 community meetings in homes, neighborhood centers and churches. There, they try to work with residents to come up with creative solutions.

One such idea came from a recent meeting of residents concerned that pay telephones in their neighborhood were being used to make drug deals.

So the CAT team began an effort with merchants to modify the telephones to limit incoming calls. Some business owners have removed pay phones.

Officers also have warned landlords their property can be seized if renters are caught selling drugs. Some landlords have taken the threat seriously.

Apparently, it has frustrated the dealers.

"In order to deal with the problem, you have to make Durham less attractive to drug dealers," said Martin. "You have to have drug treatment to decrease the demand and you have to disrupt patterns of selling and buying."

And disrupt, they have.

A patrol car is parked right next to a corner where drug dealers are known to do business. CAT members may be hiding

Staff photo by Rob Cross

Officer Tony Scott looks for a drug cache on Moreland Avenue

nearby, watching.

The dealers — who refer to the officers as "Raw Dogs" — don't visit the corner that day.

"We got a hostile response from the dealers initially," Martin said. "But as we stay there longer, it becomes like cat and mouse."

The cat-and-mouse game has resulted in more than 100 arrests. But Martin said the number of busts is not a measure of success.

Neighbors say the team has run the dealers away — for now.

"The streets are basically clean," said Juanita C. McNeil, head of the West End Neighborhood Association. "I'd say 95 percent of the traffic is gone. We know they're still there, but the officers keep them moving."

Residents have praised the team, especially Price, who said he witnessed police brutality in New York.

"This city has always been one where there has been antagonism between the black community and the police, and these officers have

gone out of their way [in] thinking of that," he said.

"They are very tactful, extremely polite and they follow the letter of the law. They just don't walk up and slam a suspect against an auto."

Price said when police officers spend time in a neighborhood and get to know the residents, they begin to care more about what happens. He said CAT members stopped by his house to check on his children one evening when he had to work late.

"These are people who have a vested interest in the community," Price said. "They don't act like thugs. They have a long-term vision."

Now the CAT team has moved to the Walltown neighborhood. But members pledge to return to West End when problems flare up. Martin said he hoped more residents will organize.

"We can't do it alone," he said. "Just policing won't do it. We're just one part of this."

Man found with 1,718 tickets

Continued from page 1B

ticket holders.

Getting into a Duke University basketball game is just as difficult. Cameron Indoor Stadium is a small arena with 9,300 seats and no one gets in to see the NCAA champions except students and season-ticket holders.

Wolfpack fans have it a little easier. Only about 50 percent of N.C. State University home games are sold out. But don't count on getting in to see an arch-rival like Duke or Carolina. Tickets to those games go first.

The huge demand and tight market breeds scalping — illegally selling tickets for more than $3 above face value — and encourages theft.

The Carolina ticket heist was the largest in Triangle basketball history. Pope was arrested and charged with possession of stolen property.

Police said they think he stole the tickets while at his job at Lassiter Pre-Sort, a Raleigh mailsorting company that contracts with UNC-CH.

The tickets carried a face value of $25,770. But the illegal scalping of the tickets — especially for games featuring more than one Triangle team — could have brought in much more.

"For the Duke and Carolina games, I've heard prices can run as high as $100 each," said John Shafer, ticket manager at NCSU. "This guy had 1,700 from Carolina? Boy, I hope he didn't get any of ours."

Monday, November 9, 1992 •   Raleigh, N.C.

SWAT training arms police facing rising crime

BY JOBY WARRICK
Staff writer

In Lt. A.C. Webster's line of work, death is a silent and ever-present partner. If he does his job just right, someone may get killed. If he makes a mistake, several people could die.

Webster works for the Durham County Sheriff's Department as part of Special Weapons and Tactics group commonly known

as a SWAT team. He's paid to be able put a .308-caliber bullet through a doughnut-size target from 200 yards — and never miss.

The job requires steel nerves, quick reflexes and unfailing accuracy. Webster knows that in a hostage situation, the difference between success and tragedy is often measured in seconds and centimeters.

Skills like his are in heavy demand in North Carolina these

days, as police rely increasingly on SWAT teams to battle a new class of heavily armed and violent criminals. The State Bureau of Investigation's three squads are busier than ever, and even small towns are sending officers to school for special training in weapons, tactics and surveillance.

At the same time, the squads themselves are coming under scrutiny, especially in the wake of

three violent confrontations in the past six weeks. The dramatic and deadly endings to armed standoffs in Oxford, Oak City and Durham won both praise and criticism for the police teams involved.

Law enforcement experts last week refused to criticize specific episodes, and they said North Carolina SWAT teams generally are well-trained and often perform heroically under life-threat-

ening conditions.

But are all SWAT squads trained as well as they should be? It's a hard question to answer, and for reasons that some officials find troubling.

There are no statewide controls on SWAT teams, no uniform guidelines for selecting members, no minimum standards for equipment and training and no standards.

See TRAINING, page 3B

Training helps police save lives

Continued from page 10

dard procedures for handling a crisis.

Although most SWAT units appear to do an excellent job across the board, standards vary from department to department, experts say. In smaller towns, training opportunities and equipment sometimes are limited by economic constraints.

With so many new SWAT teams around, some officials are arguing that all new recruits meet standardized training requirements, either within their own departments or as part of a state-run program. Such a "SWAT basic training" course is being launched for the first time in April at the N.C. Justice Academy in Salemburg.

"Police departments do the best they can with limited funds, but they need to be training every month," said Peggy Schaefer, an instructor coordinator for the state-run Academy.

While praising SWAT teams in Raleigh and Durham as models of professionalism, Schaefer says the overall lack of standardized training worries her "not because of the civil liability issues, but because I worry that some officers might not make it."

The issue has surfaced only recently in North Carolina, because, until a few years ago, only a few major cities had their own SWAT teams.

The first SWAT squad was established in Los Angeles in the 1960s, and other major cities gradually adopted the concept. But in the 1980s, a surge in drug-related crime prompted medium-sized and even smaller police departments to consider developing their own programs.

"What's dictating this trend is the increase in violence and the use of more powerful and sophisticated weapons by criminals," said Thomas Lusby, assistant agent in charge of the FBI headquarters in Charlotte. "Police today must be highly trained and mobile."

In the Triangle, in addition to Raleigh and Durham, Chapel Hill has had a Special Emergency Response Team since 1982. Even Garner, population 15,000, considered starting one.

At the N.C. Justice Academy, the first-ever SWAT training session in May drew 390 officers from 91 departments and agencies. And Schaefer said there's a waiting list for future classes.

"More and more teams are starting to form because it's really getting scary out there," she said. "There are more dangerous weapons around and criminals who are willing to use them."

The larger squads, meanwhile, are bigger and busier than ever. Raleigh's three Special Enforcement Unit squads have been working overtime in recent months because of increasing drug-related crime and a host of additional duties — including providing security for visiting presidential candidates. They still must find time to squeeze in grueling workouts and monthly training sessions with a wide array of weapons, including rifles, shotguns and MP5 submachine guns.

"It's a lot more complicated, and the training is a lot more extensive than people realize,"

said Capt. L.W. Godwin of the unit.

The SBI's three seven-man teams are having a record year, racing to hostage situations and armed standoffs across the state.

"It's basically been on the increase for the past several months," said Cuyler L. Windham, SBI senior assistant direc-

Steel nerves, quick reflexes and unfailing accuracy were required when Durham SWAT team members were called in to handle a hostage situation at Duke University last month.

tor. "On average we're now involved at least once a month. And that's just the ones we're called to help with."

SBI teams were involved in two of the three widely publicized confrontations in recent weeks. On Oct. 12, they were summoned to Oak City after a gunman shot and killed a county sheriff and

holed up inside a bank with two hostages. The standoff ended the next day when officers shot and wounded the gunman. An SBI agent inadvertently shot and killed one of the hostages.

On Oct. 17, the SBI served as a backup to Durham SWAT teams after Guilford County Jail escapee Ricky Lamont Coffin took hostages in a Duke University medical building. A Durham police sniper shot and killed Coffin with a single rifle shot to the head.

On Sept. 21, police in Oxford stormed the home of a mentally ill woman after she fired a pistol at a police officer who was trying to take her to a mental hospital. The officer was spared serious injury because of a bulletproof vest, but the woman, Thelma D. Talbott, died Oct. 26 from burns she suffered when police lobbed tear gas canisters into her home.

The deaths in all three episodes drew complaints from relatives and others who think police acted rashly or were too quick to use deadly force. In the Oak City case, Attorney General Lacy Thornburg has asked the FBI to investigate the shooting.

Other officials, though, say the criticisms show that many people don't understand the incredible pressures under which SWAT teams must operate.

"They have to make a decision in a split-second that people will be Monday-morning quarterbacking and perhaps litigating for the next 10 years," said Webster of the Durham County Sheriff's Department.

Lusby, the FBI agent, said he thinks the Oak City and Durham incidents were "handled in an appropriate fashion," given the circumstances. And SBI assistant director Ray Eastman said no amount of training can prevent occasional tragedies such as the accidental death in Oak City.

"We're very sorry about the way that turned out, but we support our men, who were working under very strenuous conditions," Eastman said. "Our ultimate goal is always to get the hostages out safely."

Another goal is to get the officers out safely, and that's one of the main reasons for the new SWAT "basic training" course that the N.C. Justice Academy will offer.

If Schaefer has her way, all candidates for SWAT duty in North Carolina eventually will have to take such a course before starting their new jobs. She says the training could help save not only hostages' lives but those of police officers as well.

"I want every officer to be able to go home at night, so I want all of them to have the very best training they can," she said.

"To me, that's more important than whether the bad guy goes home at night."

CHAPTER 8

Specialized Work Assignment: Selective Enforcement Tactical Team (S.E.T.T.)

The Struggle to Fit In

After becoming a member of the **Selective Enforcement Tactical Team (S.E.T.T.)**, I found myself navigating new dynamics and relationships within the unit. While I had earned my place on the team through hard work and training, I felt a growing pressure to fit in with the group, particularly with some of the same individuals who later became members of the C.A.T. Team or others who were friends with these individuals.

At the time, I considered that adapting to the team's culture might help me be accepted to feel like I truly belonged. But in the process of trying to fit in, I began to compromise what I knew to be right.

Compromising My Values

I followed the crowd, even when those actions conflicted with my values. I ignored my better judgment and aligned myself with the group, rationalizing my choices as part of "being a team player." But deep down, I knew this wasn't me.

Looking back, I realize how much I had jeopardized – not just my integrity but also my sense of self. Compromising my principles made me feel uneasy and out of alignment with the values that had begun to guide me. It wasn't long before I came to a pivotal realization: this wasn't the path I was meant to walk. It was sometime shortly after this experience and before I became a C.A.T.T. member that I accepted the *Call* to become a preacher. I was licensed to preach under the *Under-Shepherd*, Pastor Dr. W.C. Turner Jr.

Lessons Learned

The experience taught me some of the most important lessons of my career – and my life.

- **Be yourself.** I learned that trying to be someone else, simply to gain acceptance, is never worth the cost. Authenticity is a foundation that should never be sacrificed.

- **Stand firm in your values.** The compromises I made, however brief, served as a painful reminder of how easily one can be led astray when trying to fit in. From that point forward, I resolved never to again let anyone persuade me to go against my beliefs.

- **Fitting in isn't the way.** Seeking acceptance through compromise may seem like an easy solution, but it's ultimately hollow and fleeting. True respect and belonging come from staying true to who you are.

Moving Forward

These lessons stayed with me throughout the rest of my career. While the time I spent on the S.E.T. Team was challenging in many ways, it also shaped me into a stronger, more self-assured person. It reminded me of the importance of integrity – not just in how we interact with others but in how we live with ourselves. At the end of the day, I learned that being authentic and unwavering in my principles would always lead to the right path, even if that path was more difficult to walk.

Throughout my career, I would be asked by someone from the public, "Is being a Police Officer hard?" My short response was, "No… It's some of the people who I have to work with that makes things hard."

Joining the S.E.T. Team

As a result of my physical resilience during the academy and the reputation I had built as a solid officer who made strong arrests, I applied to become a member of the Selective Enforcement Tactical Team (S.E.T.T.). This was a pivotal step in my career, as the S.E.T. Team was an elite unit within the Durham Police Department, tasked with handling high-risk situations that went beyond the scope of patrol officers.

Being selected for the S.E.T.T team required not only exceptional physical abilities but also a specific mindset – one prepared to deal with the intense demands of the job and the challenges of high-stakes operations. The training was rigorous, designed to weed out those who might not be suited for the unique pressures of the role.

For me, being chosen to work with S.E.T.T. was an honor, a recognition of both my skills and my dedication to the job.

Training in Georgia

The training to become a S.E.T. Team member was two weeks and took place at a specialized facility in Gainesville, Georgia (Institute of Public Service). It was an intense program that tested us physically, mentally, and emotionally.

The training covered a host of subjects and scenarios, equipping us with the knowledge and skills required for tactical operations. Some of the key areas we focused on included:

- **Tactical Operations:** We were trained in techniques for entering high-risk environments, such as building clearings, hostage situations, and serving high-risk warrants. This training emphasized precision, communication, and teamwork.

- **Firearms Proficiency:** Advanced weapons training was a significant component, ensuring that we could operate a range of firearms with accuracy and confidence under pressure.

- **Physical Conditioning:** The physical demands of the job were reinforced with intense conditioning exercises, pushing our endurance and strength to new limits.

- **Scenario-Based Drills:** Realistic simulations prepared us for the unpredictable nature of high-risk operations, challenging us to think quickly and act decisively.

The Mindset of a S.E.T. Team Member

Beyond the physical and technical aspects, the training emphasized the mentality required to succeed as a S.E.T. Team member. This mindset involved staying calm under pressure, maintaining situational awareness, and making split-second decisions that could mean the difference between success and failure – or life and death! Not everyone was cut out for this kind of work. It required a combination of physical fitness, mental toughness, and emotional stability that went beyond the demands of standard patrol duties.

Reflections on the Experience

Completing the S.E.T. Team training and earning my place in the unit was a significant milestone in my career. It not only validated my skills and capabilities but also reinforced my commitment to excellence in law enforcement.

While my time with S.E.T.T. was challenging and, at times, fraught with its own set of struggles, the experience left an indelible mark on me as an officer and as a person. It prepared me for the challenges that lay ahead and served as a foundation for my later work with C.A.T.T. and beyond.

In this chapter, I will share a little insight into the tactical operations and experiences that shaped my time on the S.E.T. Team, offering insights into the unique demands and lessons of this elite unit.

The Reality of Policing Versus Hollywood

For many people, their understanding of law enforcement comes from what they see on television or in the movies. Shows and films often depict officers as action heroes, leaping from car chases to shootouts, with every case neatly resolved by the end of the episode. These portrayals are crafted to entertain, with stories embellished and made colorful to captivate their viewers.

While there are moments in the life and day of an officer that could very well be pulled from a movie or TV script, much of law enforcement is far from what you see on screen. The reality of policing is more nuanced, less glamorous, and often more complex than Hollywood would have you believe.

The S.E.T. Team: A Rare Exception

When it comes to specialized units like the **Selective Enforcement Tactical Team (S.E.T.T.)** – better understood by most as **SWAT** – there is a bit more truth to what you see on television. The gear, the tactics, and the high-stakes operations portrayed in movies and shows can be surprisingly accurate in many cases.

If you've watched a show or movie where officers are:

- Dressed in tactical gear, helmets, and body armor,
- Breaking down doors with sledgehammers or battering rams,
- Using stun grenades (flashbangs) to disorient suspects,
- Rappelling down buildings or conducting high-risk vehicle extractions and so on.

These are indeed things that S.E.T. Team members are trained to do – and occasionally called upon to execute.

However, it's important to emphasize that such operations are rare. They are reserved for the most critical and high-risk situations where no other options are viable. While these moments may grab headlines or dominate the plotlines of action movies, they represent a small fraction of what S.E.T. Team members actually do.

Preserving Life: The Ultimate Goal

In real-life law enforcement, particularly in a well-trained agency, the ultimate goal of any operation is to preserve life. Taking the life of an individual is never the desired outcome, even in situations where force is necessary.

To this end, every step is taken, and every effort is made to:

- **Preserve life:** Officers are trained to de-escalate situations whenever possible, using tactics that minimize the risk of harm to everyone involved.

- **Protect property:** Avoiding unnecessary damage is a key consideration, even in high-stakes situations.

- **Ensure community safety:** Tactical call-outs are carefully planned to limit risks to innocent bystanders and the surrounding community.

A well-trained team approaches every operation with precision, care, and a mindset rooted in protection – not destruction. This commitment to preserving life is a cornerstone of the S.E.T. Team's mission.

The Rare and the Real

While Hollywood loves to focus on the drama and danger of specialized units like SWAT, the reality is far more measured. The use of tactical teams is rare, and for good reason. These teams are a critical tool in law enforcement, but they are deployed only when absolutely necessary.

So, the next time you see a dramatic SWAT operation on television or in a movie, know that while some elements may be accurate, they represent only a mere fraction of the work that goes into keeping communities safe. The real work of law enforcement, including S.E.T. Team members, is often less about the spectacle and more about the preparation, strategy, and restraint that ensures everyone makes it home safely.

The Roles and Responsibilities of a S.E.T.T. Member

As a member of the Durham Police Department's Selective Enforcement Tactical Team (S.E.T.T.), our training went beyond tactical operations. Also among the specialized training we received was *Executive Protection Training*, preparing us to provide security for high-profile individuals visiting the city. This was just one of the many skill sets we developed to handle a wide range of situations.

On a day-to-day basis, our responsibilities as S.E.T. Team members varied, from serving warrants and other tasks that DPD deemed necessary, but they do, at times, include high-stakes tasks that required precision, planning, and teamwork.

Drug Raids and Search Warrants

One of our primary responsibilities was conducting drug raids, where we were tasked with forcefully gaining entry into properties suspected of housing illegal drugs, firearms, fugitives, or other criminal activity.

These operations were never approached lightly! Each raid or forceful entry was carefully and intentionally planned to minimize risks and ensure success. The process often involved obtaining a search warrant, which required us (rather, the lead Investigator) to present solid evidence and detailed information to a judge. The judge would then determine whether the warrants were justified and valid based on the information presented by the officer.

Executing these warrants required not just physical skill but also mental acuity. We had to be prepared for anything, from uncooperative suspects to hidden threats within the property. Or those who may be on the property, such as children who presented no danger to law enforcement.

Barricades and Hostage Situations

In addition to drug raids, the S.E.T. Team was also responsible for responding to barricade situations. These incidents typically involved fugitives or wanted individuals barricading themselves inside their homes, refusing to surrender.

When dealing with barricaded suspects, our approach was methodical and deliberate. The goal was always to resolve the situation peacefully, but we were prepared to act swiftly and decisively if necessary.

Another responsibility we sometimes faced was addressing hostage situations. These high-stakes scenarios required close coordination with hostage negotiators, who often worked separately from the S.E.T. Team but alongside us during critical moments. While negotiations took place, the S.E.T. Team remained on standby, ready to intervene if talks broke down and force became necessary.

Honoring police service

Staff photos by Gary Allen

Durham Police Chief Jackie McNeil speaks during an award presentation by the Durham chapter of the Veterans of Foreign Wars. Wilbur Davis of the VFW, left, presented the police department's Selective Enforcement Team with an award for outstanding devotion and dedication. Representatives of the VFW touted the team's contribution to law enforcement in the city and praised members for their actions in recent incidents, including a hostage situation at Duke University in the fall. That volatile incident ended when a member of the unit shot the hostage-taker with a single shot from more than 50 yards away. The unit of about a dozen officers is trained for hostage situations and dangerous searches.

A Hostage Situation

I will provide shortly one hostage situation where I was part of the S.E.T. Team's response. While some details of this specific incident will remain limited, I can say that it was one of those moments that required every ounce of our training, preparation, and focus!

Hostage situations are inherently unpredictable! Every decision, every move we made, had the potential to either de-escalate or escalate the situation. The lives of both the hostages and the suspect were at stake, and the weight of that responsibility was never lost on us!

The resolution of this particular incident highlighted the importance of teamwork, strategy, and restraint. It was a reminder of why the S.E.T. Team exists: to handle the most challenging and dangerous situations with professionalism and care.

Reflections on the S.E.T. Team

Being part of the S.E.T. Team was a demanding but rewarding experience. The diversity of tasks, from drug raids to hostage situations, required us to remain adaptable and focused at all times. Each operation reinforced the importance of preparation, precision, and the preservation of life.

While many people see SWAT teams as action-oriented units, the truth is that much of our work involved preventing harm and resolving conflicts peacefully whenever possible. Every operation, no matter how high the stakes, was approached with one ultimate goal: to protect and serve the people of Durham.

Hostage Situation at Duke South Hospital (Duke University)

While working with the C.A.T. Team, I found myself involved in a high-stakes incident that would call upon the training and coordination of the S.E.T. Team. It began with a radio transmission that immediately caught my attention while I was patrolling in West Durham on Moorhead Avenue.

The 911 dispatch provided information about a car chase initiated by the Highway Patrol. An individual was fleeing law enforcement while actively firing a weapon from his car. The chase was headed toward Durham, and every officer listening knew that this situation could escalate quickly!

A Dangerous Turn

The chase culminated at Duke South Hospital, where the suspect abandoned the car and ran into the building. He made his way inside, entered an office, and took hostages. The danger was clear: a gunman in a densely populated hospital, with lives at immediate risk!

The S.E.T. Team was called out to respond to the crisis. As a member of the team, I was among those dispatched to the scene.

On Scene at Duke South

Upon arrival, other team members joined me at the southeast corner of Duke South Hospital… at the time this event was unfolding, I was only a couple of miles from Duke. The situation was tense! Every move we made had to be calculated, every strategy deliberate. After dawning our tactical gear, we – only a team of three of us would be entering the building; we coordinated our efforts while ensuring that no additional harm came to the hostages or bystanders within the hospital. This was an intense and urgent situation!

As we took up positions, our skilled sniper moved into place, positioning himself strategically to deal with the threat if the situation escalated further! The presence of a sniper highlighted the seriousness of the incident; if negotiations failed or if the suspect posed an imminent threat to the hostages or the public, we were prepared to act decisively!

Reflections on the Incident

Hostage situations like this are what SWAT or S.E.T. Teams train for, but they are never routine. The stakes are incredibly high, and the lives of innocent people depend on our ability to remain calm, focused, and professional.

This incident at Duke South Hospital reminds me of the critical importance of teamwork, communication, and preparation in law enforcement. While I will not provide the full details of the resolution to address this matter, I can say that the efforts of every team member that day were guided by one goal: to protect lives and quickly resolve the matter as the situation/suspect dictated things.

The Gravity of the Role

Incidents like the Duke South hostage situation serve as a sobering reminder of the unpredictable nature of law enforcement. They also reinforce the importance of specialized training and the role of teams like S.E.T.T. in managing crises that go beyond the scope of routine patrol work.

For me, this experience underscored why the work we did on the S.E.T. Team mattered. It wasn't about glory or recognition; it was about rising to the occasion in moments of uncertainty and danger, doing everything in our power to ensure the safety of the community we served.

A Tense Standoff

As the situation at Duke South Hospital escalated, three of us on the S.E.T. Team staged outside the barricaded door where the suspect had taken hostages. The hallway was silent except for the sounds of tension – muffled orders and the knowledge that on the other side of that door, lives hung in the balance!

The suspect remained an active and imminent threat! Before we had taken position in the hallway, from inside the office, I believe the suspect had fired his weapon out the window, endangering not only the hostages but also those outside the building. The situation demanded immediate action, and the command was given to neutralize the threat!

The Shot

Moments later, the shot rang out! I had not been informed beforehand by the S.E.T.T. member in charge that our sniper had been given the green light to neutralize the threat, as I should have been alerted! Stationed outside of the door where the hostages were, I then heard the shot echo through the hallway! It was merely assumed that the threat had been neutralized! I was not informed otherwise; now it was time for us to gain entry and secure the room!

What unfolded next is something that has stayed with me all these years, a moment that still troubles me deeply!

A Troubling Command

The S.E.T. Team member in charge of our team in the hallway was the same individual who, as I later learned from Robert, had opposed my joining the S.E.T. Team. Per training and protocol, he and the officer positioned on the left side of the hallway – the same side as the door handle – were responsible for making entry. This setup ensured that the officers nearest to the door could quickly and efficiently breach it while minimizing exposure to danger!

However, after the shot was fired by our sniper, the officer in charge issued an unexpected and troubling command: he ordered me to cross the hallway and enter the "deadly funnel," the high-risk zone, directly in front of the door!

While the deadly funnel is a critical area during tactical operations, it is also the most dangerous position, as it exposes the officer to potential gunfire or other threats from inside the room.

Despite my concerns, I followed the command. I crossed the hallway, now I was in front of the other two team members and became the point man. I advanced toward the door with the other two team members behind me. I positioned myself in front of the door and forced it open; it had been barricaded!

What should have occurred: After the shot was fired, the team member in charge, who was now positioned behind the other team member, those two should have immediately preceded to the door! I would have then followed in behind them. Instead, I was commanded to become the point man while the S.E.T. Team member in charge took up the rear... go figure!

Entry and Resolution

Once inside, being the first to gain entry, I saw that the threat had indeed been neutralized; I handcuffed him as training required. The suspect had been fatally shot, but the hostages were unharmed. As per protocol, we proceeded to secure the room, ensuring that the hostages were safe and the scene was under control.

While the operation was ultimately successful – no harm came to the hostages – the incident regarding the command given me by either the fearful S.E.T. Team member in charge or whatever his motivation may have been... left an indelible mark on me!

Reflections

The events of that day have stayed with me, not only because of the life-and-death stakes but also because of the troubling dynamic within our team. The officer in charge, the same person who had voiced opposition to my joining the S.E.T. Team, had deviated from protocol in a way that placed me in unnecessary danger!

To this day, I question his motivations. Was it a matter of poor judgment under pressure, or was it something more deliberate? Whatever the case, I knew in that moment that I had to maintain my professionalism, focus on the task at hand, and protect the lives of the hostages.

This experience reinforced a lesson I had learned earlier in my career: to stand firm in who I am and to trust in my training, regardless of the challenges or dynamics around me. It also underscored the importance of accountability and integrity within specialized units like S.E.T.T., where trust and teamwork are essential to success.

Caught in the Crossfire

No amount of training could have prepared me for what happened on one late evening. As a C.A.T.T. officer and S.E.T. member, I was patrolling the Fayetteville Street Housing Development when I noticed a group of young African American men, likely in their teens and twenties, standing together in the parking lot.

Typically, when encountering such gatherings, I would employ a specific tactic: pulling up in front of the group and observing their behavior to see who flinched, who began to walk away, or who otherwise acted suspiciously. These reactions often provided clues about whether any of them were engaged in illegal activity.

But this time, I decided on a different approach. Instead of stopping immediately, I chose to drive past the group and park my vehicle on Fayetteville Street, near Merrick Street. From there, I got out of my car and walked in behind the group, hoping to quietly observe their activity more closely.

Gunfire Erupts

Moments after positioning myself on the hill behind them, a multitude of gunfire erupted! The shots weren't just random; they were exchanged with terrifying precision and ferocity! I quickly realized that the men I had been observing were firing at a group across the street (Umstead St.) and that the other group was returning fire just as aggressively! I could also hear the bullets ricocheting off objects they struck!

It was chaos! The gunfire was deafening, the air thick with tension and danger. The two groups were locked in what could only be described as a gun battle! Later, my investigation revealed that the opposing group was from McDougald Terrace – The Mac, and the group I had been standing behind was from the Fayetteville Street Housing Development.

11/05/2007

Taking Cover

As the shots continued to ring out, I instinctively sought concealment on a nearby porch, doing what was reasonable to protect myself. My position gave me a moment of safety but also a vantage point to assess the situation.

I immediately called out for backup, radioing in the gravity of what was unfolding: "10 18 Shots fired! Multiple shooters! Be careful when approaching!" My message carried an urgent warning for the responding officers, emphasizing the seriousness and unpredictability of the situation!

The Aftermath

Eventually, backup arrived. However, due to the blaring sirens of police units that were headed my way, the gunfire had ceased. One vehicle involved in the incident fled the scene but was stopped on Pettigrew Street. Though I don't recall the precise outcome of the stop, I do remember that the individuals in the vehicle were identified as residents of McDougald Terrace.

The scene left a lasting impression on me. It was a stark reminder of the very real and dangerous conditions we faced as officers. While we trained extensively for high-risk situations, nothing truly prepares you for the moment when you're caught in the crossfire of a gun battle.

The Fayetteville Street projects were quiet now, but the chaos of the shootout still rang in my mind. The aftermath of gunfire isn't just in the physical evidence left behind – casings on the ground, shattered windows, and the echoes of violence. It's in the weight that one can carry afterward. As a police officer, you learn to live with it, but it never leaves you!

Even now, in retirement, as I indicated earlier, my mind is never truly at rest! That same alertness I carried on patrol follows me as a civilian, a constant hum of vigilance. I've often reflected on the lives I've touched and, in some cases, the lives I've saved literally or in other ways. There's the child I mentioned earlier, but there are also two other moments that stand out to me – moments where I clearly saved lives, albeit in very different circumstances.

The first happened during training in Georgia. I was there to become a member of the Selective Enforcement Team. We were practicing rappelling off a six to eight-story building, a high-stakes environment requiring focus and discipline. As I stood in line waiting for my turn, I noticed a trainee creeping dangerously close to the edge of the tower. Something about his body language struck me – perhaps he was experiencing a measure of fear; therefore, his mind was not focused.

Next, what immediately stood out to me was that he didn't have his rappelling rope secured to his harness! We were either practicing the rappelling tactics called "Australian or Jump Rappelling."

The officer was facing forward with his back towards us, inches away from disaster!

I screamed, "Get him!" just as he was about to step/leap off the edge! A trainer reached out and pulled him back in time. Seconds later, it would have likely been a fatal fall. Observance and quick reaction saved his life that day, and it was a stark reminder of the unpredictability of our profession.

The second moment came in an entirely different setting: during a worship service at my church. It was a typical Sunday morning, but my attention was drawn to a young woman standing at the front of the congregation. Even from several feet away, with people sitting between us and beside her, I could see something was wrong. She was choking!

I didn't hesitate! Without saying a word to anyone, I moved quickly to where she stood, positioned myself behind her, and performed the Heimlich maneuver! One firm thrust was all it took to dislodge the mint candy that had been blocking her airway. She gasped for air, and the crisis was over almost as soon as it began!

Once a cop, always a cop, that instinct to act – to observe, assess, and respond – never truly leaves you. Whether it's a dangerous moment during training or a life-threatening emergency in a church, vigilance is part of who we are.

Reflections

This experience (the shoot-out) in Fayetteville Housing Development underscored the unpredictability of policing in high-crime areas. Despite my training and instincts, I found myself thrust into a life-threatening situation that required quick thinking and decisive action.

It also reminded me of the importance of vigilance and adaptability. Sometimes, even the best tactics and preparation can't prevent danger, but they can help you navigate it.

Above all, this incident reinforced the gravity of my role as a police officer: to protect and serve, even in the face of unimaginable risks. Moments like these tested not only my skills but also my resolve – and they left me with lessons I carried with me for the rest of my career.

Resigning from the S.E.T. Team

The hostage takeover at Duke South Hospital, while a critical moment in my career, came on the heels of an equally intense and dangerous situation: the shootout at Fayetteville Street and Merrick Street. Both incidents tested my training, resolve, and ability to perform under extreme pressure.

However, the hostage incident left me with a lingering sense of disillusionment, particularly due to the actions of the team member, who issued an order that violated protocol and put me at unnecessary risk. This breach of trust, coupled with the overall dynamics within the S.E.T. Team, left a bitter taste in my mouth!

I had already felt the tension of not fitting in with the group, and this experience only solidified my belief that it was time to step away. The combination of questionable leadership, strained relationships, and my growing unease with the unit's dynamics led me to a difficult but necessary decision: to resign from my position as a S.E.T. Team member.

Returning to the C.A.T. Team

After resigning from the SET team, I returned to my work with the C.A.T. Team, where I continued my efforts to combat street-level drug activity and make a positive impact in Durham's neighborhoods.

For a time, I was able to refocus on the work I believed in – building rapport with the community, conducting targeted patrols, and addressing the drug epidemic that plagued our city. However, as I've shared earlier, my tenure with the C.A.T. Team eventually came to an end following the incident involving my supervisor and the challenges I faced in standing up for what was right.

Back to Uniform Patrol

After leaving the C.A.T. Team, I returned to Uniform Patrol, where my journey as a law enforcement officer came full circle. This transition allowed me to step back into a familiar role, continuing to serve the community while navigating the lessons and experiences I had gained from my time on both the C.A.T. Team and S.E.T. Teams.

A Step Toward Detective Work

Despite the setbacks and challenges I faced, these experiences were pivotal in shaping the next phase of my career. My return to Uniform Patrol became a stepping stone toward achieving another goal: becoming a detective. This move allowed me to focus on a different aspect of law enforcement, one that required investigative skills, attention to detail, and a commitment to justice that had been forged through years of fieldwork.

Reflection II

Resigning from the SET team was not an easy decision, but it was a necessary one. It marked the end of one chapter and the beginning of another, allowing me to realign with my values and refocus on the work that mattered most to me.

Every experience – both good and challenging – helped prepare me for the path ahead. From the chaos of tactical operations to the daily grind of uniform patrol, each role brought new lessons, new challenges, and new opportunities to serve my community with integrity and purpose.

11/05/2007

CHAPTER 9

Detective T.L. Scott

What Makes a Good Detective

The transition from uniformed patrol to detective work is one that requires a solid foundation built on years of experience. An officer aspiring to become a great detective should have spent several years on patrol, honing the essential skills needed to excel in investigations.

These foundational skills include:

- **Detailed Report Writing:** A good patrol officer understands the importance of crafting comprehensive, accurate, and detailed reports. These reports often form the basis for investigations and can be critical in ensuring justice is served.

- **Effective Questioning:** The ability to question witnesses and potential suspects while extracting relevant information is an art that must be mastered over time. This skill is indispensable for detectives.

- **Attention to Detail:** Patrol officers who develop a keen eye for details, both in their reports and on the scene, are better equipped to transition into investigative work, where every piece of evidence can make or break a case.

- **Community Rapport:** Perhaps one of the most critical elements is the relationship an officer builds with the community. Officers who have established trust and respect within the neighborhoods they patrol often find themselves better positioned as detectives. These relationships can lead to invaluable tips, cooperation from witnesses, and a deeper understanding of the community's dynamics.

The Role of Community Support

Policing and detective work, in particular, requires the support of the community. Citizens are often the key to solving cases, and a detective who has built strong relationships in the neighborhoods they once patrolled can leverage those connections to gather information.

For example, when returning to a community as a detective, a respected officer may find that people are more willing to share what they know, help identify suspects, or provide critical leads. This trust is earned, not given! Officers who take the time to serve and protect with integrity, treating citizens with respect, often reap the benefits of those efforts when they transition into detective work.

The Reality of Detective Work

While television shows and movies glamorize the role of a detective, the reality is far from the dramatic, fast-paced stories often depicted on screen.

Detective work is intense, demanding, and often thankless. It requires patience, persistence, and a relentless commitment to uncovering the truth. Detectives spend countless hours poring over evidence, conducting interviews, coordinating with other agencies, and chasing leads – many of which don't pan out.

In a city as large and busy as Durham, the workload can be overwhelming.

- **Cases Never Stop Coming In:** There is no shortage of crimes to investigate, and the flow of new cases can feel relentless.

- **Round-the-Clock Commitment:** For detectives, the work doesn't stop at the end of a shift. It's not uncommon to work late into the night or be called in during off-hours to respond to urgent developments.

- **The Pressure to Solve Cases:** Detectives often face immense pressure from their department, the public, and themselves to solve cases quickly and effectively.

A Calling, Not a Job

Despite the challenges, those who succeed as detectives are often driven by a sense of purpose. They understand the weight of their responsibility – to bring justice to victims, to hold criminals accountable, and to ensure the safety of their communities. When this is done well, only then is a detective possibly rewarded with a "Thank you" from the family or individual they served. Or, is perhaps acknowledged from in-house for a job well done.

The work may not come with the glamour or recognition that Hollywood portrays, but it is profoundly meaningful. Great detectives are those who embrace the grind, approach every case with determination, and never lose sight of the impact their work has on the lives of others.

Closing Reflections on Detective Work

I don't think it is necessary for me to share the specific cases I investigated during my time as a detective for you to grasp the nature of this work. I believe I have shared and/or will share sufficient details to give you a clear understanding of what detective work entails – the intensity, complexity, and dedication it requires.

Uniformed patrol officers play a crucial role in the investigative process. Depending on the nature of the crime, they may be able to handle the case from start to finish. They gather evidence, interview witnesses, apprehend suspects, and even question them, often bringing swift resolution to incidents.

However, there are many cases where the crime is too egregious or where insufficient information prevents an arrest during the initial response. In such instances, the case is handed off to the *Detective Division*, where the true grind of investigative work begins.

The Work of a Detective

Detective work is more than just solving puzzles or piecing together clues. It is an exhaustive process that demands both mental acuity and relentless effort.

Some of the key responsibilities include:

- **Receiving Well-Written Reports:** Detectives rely on patrol officers to provide accurate and detailed reports. A poorly written report can hinder the entire investigation.

- **Overseeing Evidence Handling:** Ensuring that evidence is collected, processed, and properly documented is critical. Detectives must confirm that the correct evidence has been turned in and, when necessary, revisit the crime scene to uncover additional clues.

- **Crime Scene Analysis:** Upon visiting or revisiting a crime scene, detectives assess the scene, draw conclusions about what occurred, and provide instructions for further evidence collection. Their observations can shape the direction of the investigation.

- **Processing Evidence:** Detectives often send or have sent evidence to labs, follow up on the results, and integrate findings into their case.

- **Building a Case:** This involves reviewing all gathered information, talking with witnesses, consulting with the DA's office and attorneys involved in the case, and preparing for court proceedings.

- **Court Testimony:** Standing on the witness stand and presenting the case in court is a critical aspect of detective work. Detectives must ensure that their findings are clear, credible, and admissible, helping to bring resolution for victims and justice for the community.

The sheer amount of work involved in detective work cannot be overstated. It is grueling and relentless, requiring long hours, critical thinking, and meticulous attention to detail. But for those who embrace the challenge, the rewards, though not always immediate, can be deeply satisfying.

A Conversation with Sergeant A.J. Carter

One moment that stands out from my time in the detective bureau is a conversation I had with Sergeant A.J. Carter, a man I greatly respected. At the time, Carter had been working specifically in the homicide division – one of the most demanding areas of law enforcement.

Later, when Carter was promoted to sergeant and returned to patrol work. It was during this transition that we spoke, and his words left a profound impression on me.

"I didn't realize the amount of stress I was under as an investigator until I was promoted and went back to the streets," he told me.

His reflection struck me deeply. It underscored the unique pressures detectives face, pressures that often go unnoticed in the moment but weigh heavily over time. The constant influx of cases, the emotional toll of dealing with victims and their families, and the relentless pursuit of justice – it all adds up! For Carter, stepping away from those responsibilities provided a clarity he hadn't experienced while in the thick of it.

Gratitude for the Role

While detective work is far from the glamorous portrayal often seen in movies and television, it is profoundly meaningful. It requires dedication, resilience, and an unwavering commitment to seeking truth and justice.

Looking back, I am grateful for the time I spent in the detective bureau. The experiences taught me invaluable lessons about perseverance, integrity, and the importance of community in achieving justice. Even now, years later, I carry those lessons with me, and I remain deeply respectful of the detectives who continue to do this challenging but essential work.

I reflect on the ending of my journey in law enforcement, I think of that one question citizens would occasionally ask me: "Is policing hard?" My response, as shared earlier, was simple yet profound: "No, policing is not hard. It's the people I have to work with."

While my years in uniform and as a detective were filled with meaningful moments and opportunities to serve, as demonstrated, there were also challenges that stemmed from the working environment itself. And as I've expressed, these challenges tested my resolve and ultimately shaped the trajectory of my career. My less favorable experiences, perhaps, were unique to me. I sure hope so. Nevertheless, Ron Wiggin's experience was eerily similar to mine.

A Challenging Supervisor

During my time as a detective, I had the unfortunate experience of working under a supervisor who was, to put it mildly, challenging. The working environment they created compelled me to speak out. I brought my concerns to my commander, who listened and, apparently, investigated the matter further.

Shortly thereafter, I found myself returning to uniform patrol after this unfavorable experience. Interestingly, it seemed that my concerns were validated. Either a civilian complaint or the commander's findings or both led to the supervisor being reassigned to the streets. Eventually, that supervisor chose to resign from the Durham Police Department entirely.

Another Difficult Experience

Unfortunately, yet again, I faced challenges with leadership. Another supervisor I worked with also made the work environment difficult. As a result of my experience with this individual, I made the decision to resign from the Durham Police Department.

My Rehire: Returning to the Police Department

Though I had chosen to leave, my reputation as a dedicated officer preceded me. It wasn't long before a ranking officer reached out to encourage me to return to the department. I believe this was the same officer who had been a church member and may have inadvertently played a role in my suspension from the C.A.T. Team. Regardless, this officer paved the way for my return, and I am grateful for their encouragement and efforts!

During the brief rehiring process, I was informed by the investigator conducting my background check of a surprising development. When the investigator questioned my former supervisor – whose leadership, or lack thereof, had prompted my earlier resignation – the supervisor advised against bringing me back.

The investigator, perplexed by this response, escalated the matter to their commander. The commander overruled the former supervisor, stating, "Bring him back. We want him back." I returned to District 4, and later, I volunteered to become a desk officer. More will be said about this experience in *Chapter 10*.

Gratitude for the Road

This chapter of my journey serves as a testament to the importance of maintaining integrity and professionalism, even in the face of adversity. While the road was not always smooth, I am grateful for the opportunities I had to serve, the lessons I learned, and the people who believed in me and supported my return.

My reputation as a fine officer – a reputation built on hard work, dedication, and a commitment to doing what was right – ultimately opened doors that others sought to close. For that, I am profoundly thankful.

Just the same, I can call this God's Favor or Grace!

CHAPTER 10

Community Oriented Policing (C.O.P.), Gang Resistance Education And Training (G.R.E.A.T.), The Last of My Assignments

Diverse Work Experiences

One of the unique advantages of working within the Durham Police Department is the opportunity to explore various career paths and work experiences. The size of the agency allows officers to gain exposure to different facets of law enforcement or community service, and as you've seen from my story thus far, I've had the privilege of serving in several different roles over the years.

Two of the work experiences that I will highlight now are my time with Community Oriented Policing (C.O.P.) and Gang Resistance Education and Training (G.R.E.A.T.) programs. Both were vital initiatives designed to build trust within the community and address systemic issues at their roots, often before they escalated into larger problems.

Community-Oriented Policing (C.O.P.)

The Community-Oriented Policing (C.O.P.) program emphasized

fostering positive relationships between law enforcement and the communities we served. This approach sought to build trust, encourage open communication, and address concerns before they became major law enforcement issues.

As a C.O.P. officer, my role extended beyond traditional policing. It was about:

- Engaging with residents in a proactive, non-confrontational manner,
- Identifying the unique needs and challenges of each neighborhood, and
- Working collaboratively with community members to develop solutions that enhanced public safety.

C.O.P. work was incredibly rewarding because it allowed me to see firsthand the power of collaboration and trust. By being present, listening, and offering support, I was able to connect with people in meaningful ways that went beyond the badge.

Gang Resistance Education and Training (G.R.E.A.T.)

The **Gang Resistance Education and Training (G.R.E.A.T.)** program was another impactful initiative I had the privilege of being part of. G.R.E.A.T. was focused on preventing gang involvement among youth, helping them build resilience and make better life choices before they became entangled in criminal activity.

This program assigned me to a school where I worked directly with 6th graders, teaching them about the dangers of gang life and equipping them with the tools to resist peer pressure. I had the opportunity and privilege to be assigned to two schools: Shepherd Middle School and W.G. Pearson. My youngest son, Desmond had attended this school (Shepherd) the year before I was assigned there. W.G. Pearson was a neighborhood school in *The Old Hayti Community*, located across the street from Fayetteville Street, public housing, where I lived for a few years as a child directly across the street from the school. Some years later, after my family moved, I was also able to attend Merrick–Moore Elementary School, another school that was started by African American men, each of who were essential individuals within the development of *The Old Hayti District*... what a privilege!

Through G.R.E.A.T., I had the opportunity to:

- Serve as a mentor and role model to at-risk youth,
- Partner with educators and community leaders to create safe environments and
- Help shape the future of Durham's young people by steering them away from crime and toward positive opportunities.

Seeing the impact of this work was incredibly fulfilling! Knowing that I was helping to change the trajectory of a young person's life made all the challenges of law enforcement worthwhile.

A Microcosm of the Community

As a G.R.E.A.T. (Gang Resistance Education and Training) officer, I quickly realized that the students I worked with in various schools represented a microcosm of the community. They reflected the diverse realities of their upbringing and neighborhoods – some students excelled with the support of caring families, while others struggled due to the lack of it.

What I witnessed in the schools was both enlightening and alarming. Shepard Middle School, in particular, stood out to me. The year before, it had been voted the best middle school in the area, a beacon of success as a magnet school. Yet, just one year later, I observed things that deeply concerned me. I remember thinking and openly expressing, "If what I am seeing in this school, which at the time was perhaps the smallest middle school in Durham with a population of about 200. What do things look like in considerably large schools?"

Without going into specifics, I will simply say this, as I've often expressed over the years: I went into the schools to teach, to guide, and to mentor students. But in the end, I left, having been schooled." With the problems that I saw within Durham Public Schools over a decade ago, I can only imagine the challenges that educators now face daily… much has changed in the past 2 decades! Let me add: Our educators deserve every DOLLAR $$$ they ask for, whether they are in Durham or surrounding areas! And so do our Law Enforcement Officers!

A Choice About Promotions

Within the Durham Police Department, there are ample opportunities for career advancement. Officers can move up the ranks, becoming corporals, sergeants, lieutenants, or even commanders. These promotions offer greater responsibility and leadership opportunities, as well as the chance to shape the direction of the department.

For me, however, promotion was never my aspiration.

One of the drawbacks of promotion within the department when I was there was that officers working in specialized units – such as C.A.T.T. or even programs like C.O.P. and G.R.E.A.T. – must more often than not return to uniformed patrol when they advance to the next rank. As a corporal or sergeant, the flexibility and specialization of the previous role are traded for broader oversight responsibilities back on uniform patrol.

At the time, I had young sons, and my priorities were clear. I wanted to be present for them during their formative years – coaching their sports teams, attending their school activities, and being there for the moments that mattered most.

Prioritizing Family

Policing is a demanding career, and the long hours and unpredictable schedule can take a toll on family life. For me, the decision to remain in specialized roles rather than pursuing promotions was rooted in my commitment to my family.

I found fulfillment in my work with C.O.P., G.R.E.A.T., and other specialized units. These roles allowed me to make a difference in the community while maintaining a schedule that enabled me to be there for my sons during the years when they needed me most.

Reflections

Looking back, I have no regrets about my decision. While I chose not to climb the ranks, I was able to serve in meaningful ways that aligned with my values and priorities. I was present for my family, contributed to the betterment of my community, and found great purpose in the work I did.

For me, success wasn't defined by titles or rank – it was defined by the impact I made, both at home and in the streets of Durham. Over a decade later, from time to time, I cross paths with my former, now adult G.R.E.A.T. students. When they encounter me, they greet me with a smile and still address me as Officer Scott; with laughter, I quickly have them address me otherwise.

Then there are those whose history with me goes back much further; they will address me as "Robo-cop;" this greeting is always quite surprising! In both situations, oftentimes, someone begins our conversation with, "Do you remember when…" this or that happened? More times than not, I don't recall their story or our interaction together. Nevertheless, it is great to be acknowledged and warmly greeted by someone I served in my community. These are people who I encountered on both sides of the law.

Transitioning to a Desk Officer

As the years went by and I approached retirement, the physical and mental demands of patrol work were no longer in me. While policing requires one to be young in heart, it also demands a level of stamina and energy that is better suited to those who are young in age. With this understanding, I volunteered to become a desk officer – a role at the time many may underestimate, but that carries its own unique set of challenges and rewards.

The Role of a Desk Officer

The job of a desk officer encompasses far more than greeting people who walk through the front doors of police headquarters. It's a multifaceted role that requires patience, adaptability, and a willingness to help in countless ways.

Among my daily responsibilities were:

- Greeting visitors and issuing guest passes,
- Answering a wide variety of questions – ranging from city services to legal inquiries,
- Assisting officers with tasks as needed,
- Taking reports for certain types of incidents, and
- Logging information about vehicles that had been towed.

Daytime shifts were particularly demanding. The steady flow of visitors and the constant ringing of telephones could make the work feel overwhelming at times. But, like patrol work, the desk officer role came with a few moments of great reward – especially when it came to connecting with people who truly needed my assistance and the extra that I would provide as I continued going beyond what was required of me within my profession.

Connecting with the Community

Even as a desk officer, I carried the same mindset I had during my years on patrol: to make a positive impact wherever I could.

I especially enjoyed interacting with children. When groups of kids came in for tours of the police headquarters, I always made it a point to engage with them. I handed out stickers, shared encouraging words, and kept a stash of candy at the desk – not just for the officers but for the kids as well.

These small gestures reminded me that a police officer never stops being a police officer. Even behind a desk, I found opportunities to connect with the community and make a difference in people's lives.

Memorable Experiences

During my time as a desk officer, there were three incidents that stand out in my mind, each reflecting the unpredictability and impact of the role.

1. A Domestic Situation

One day, a woman walked into headquarters visibly upset. It was brought to my attention that she was dealing with a domestic issue involving her husband. As was my custom, I took the time to listen carefully and tried to get to the root of the problem.

After she shared what was going on, I offered her the guidance and support she needed. Her relief was evident – not just in her words of thanks but in the tears that rolled down her cheeks. In that moment, I could see how much my assistance meant to her.

2. A Shocking Confession

One late night, an African American man in his late 20s or early 30s walked into headquarters. His demeanor was cautious, his speech slow. He looked at me and said something I'll never forget:

"I just killed someone."

My immediate response was to remain calm. I instructed him to stand where he was, exited my elevated desk position, and approached him carefully. I secured him with handcuffs and called for backup.

Officers arrived shortly thereafter to take him into custody. The situation was surreal – a stark reminder of the unpredictability of law enforcement. On any given day or night, you never know what you'll encounter.

3. An Uplifting Encounter

Among the more heartwarming moments was an interaction with a woman who had visited headquarters a few times. A colleague from the records division informed me that she wanted to meet me but was too nervous to approach.

When I learned that she wanted to encourage me and thank me for my service as a law enforcement officer, I welcomed her with open arms. She was a Christian, and during our conversation, she shared how much she admired my work and my faith.

This interaction became a turning point for her. As a result of our engagement, she blossomed in her faith, becoming bold in her conversations with others and sharing her testimony freely. I still remember her name: Yvonne H. Not only do I remember her name, I've met her husband. This family is quite dear to me, especially Yvonne... what a jewel of a person!

Gratitude for the Role

My time as a desk officer proved to be a rewarding chapter in my career. While it was a shift from the adrenaline and intensity of patrol work, it offered its own set of challenges and opportunities to serve.

The Durham Police Department provided me with a career that was rich with experiences, growth, and purpose. Whether I was patrolling the streets, engaging with the community, or working behind the desk, I was always reminded of the profound privilege it is to serve and protect.

I served well; my final shift as The Bull City's Sentinel concluded on September 13, 2013. My official retirement date was April 9th, 2014.

CERTIFICATE OF COMPLETION

MAY IT BE KNOWN THAT

Tony Scott

HAS COMPLETED THE

Gang Resistance Education And Training
80-HOUR OFFICER TRAINING PROGRAM

CHAIR, NATIONAL POLICY BOARD

Friday, July 22, 2005
DATE

NATIONAL TRAINING TEAM MEMBER

GREAT DAY (AND WAY) TO RELAX

The Herald-Sun/CATHY SEITH

Tony Scott takes off his shoes to relax in the shade and read the Bible on Friday afternoon at West Point on the Eno. "I just love coming out to the Eno, to hear the birds chirping, the water crashing of the waterfall. I love the peace it gives me," Scott said. "Being out in nature away from the hustle and bustle and stress, it's healing." Scott is a Durham police officer.

CHAPTER 11

Defund the Police - What Foolishness

As I reflect on my years in law enforcement, one thing remains clear: law enforcement has evolved and changed significantly over the years. When I began my career, there was a measure of mutual respect between officers and those who committed crimes – at least in the city of Durham. This respect didn't mean we condoned crime; it meant there was a shared understanding of roles and a line that wasn't readily crossed.

Durham Police Department has always been home to some of the best-trained officers in the state. I take great pride in this. However, I also acknowledge that no system is perfect, nor person and neither was I... I had my few moments. Bad officers can be hired, good officers can make costly mistakes, and even good officers can lose their way. As I approached retirement, I began to notice a shift in this dynamic of mutual respect with officers and those they serve.

Certain incidents – both locally and nationally – have shown a negative light on policing. As I've mentioned earlier in this book, one bad officer can tarnish the reputation of an entire department. In the age of social media, such an issue can become magnified, perhaps even rightly so. The actions of a few officers are broadcast instantly and globally, shaping the public perception that can be out of proportion to reality. Or, because people really don't understand the scope and authority given to police officers, citizens are too quick to make judgments wrongly about policing matters that they are clueless about.

High-profile incidents involving law enforcement and people of color added to this strained relationship. Some of the most significant cases include:

- **Trayvon Martin (2012)**: While not directly a police shooting, this case highlighted racial tensions and questions about law enforcement and public safety.

- **Eric Garner (2014)**: Garner's death after being placed in a chokehold by NYPD officers brought police tactics and accountability under intense scrutiny.

- **Michael Brown (2014)**: Brown's death in Ferguson, Missouri, led to nationwide protests against police brutality and racial bias.

- **Tamir Rice (2014)**: A 12-year-old boy shot by police while holding a toy gun raised questions about the use of force.

- **George Floyd (2020)**: Floyd's death under the knee of a Minneapolis police officer reignited global protests and calls for reform.

These and countless other incidents have led to cries of "defund the police," police reform, and demands for greater accountability. Groups like Black Lives Matter amplified these calls, and while some of their concerns are valid, their broader agenda often diverges from practical solutions. The extreme left of the "woke" movement further exacerbates the issue by pushing the narrative that law enforcement itself is the problem.

Defunding the police, however, is sheer foolishness! Such a move would lead to chaos and anarchy, plunging our communities into problems we haven't seen in modern times. Imagine a society without law enforcement – a society where order collapses and lawlessness reigns. This is not a solution; it's a recipe for disaster!

That said, I firmly believe in accountability and transparency. Police officers must be held to the highest standards, and departments should address failures swiftly and decisively! Collaboration with the community is essential. Trust cannot be demanded; it must be earned. Officers should receive continual training to equip them with the skills and judgment necessary to serve diverse communities effectively. I'm glad to say that I served with an agency that did and continues to do just that!

To my fellow officers: Represent your departments and communities well! Remember your oath to protect and serve all! Uphold the highest standards of integrity and professionalism. Your work is vital to maintaining the fabric of our society.

And to the public: Support the officers who dedicate themselves to your safety. Critique is fair, and accountability is necessary, but demonizing the entire profession is both unjust and counterproductive.

I salute my fellow officers, past and present.
Thank you for your service!

Durham Police Pay Tribute To Slain Officers

By GREGORY CHILDRESS
Herald staff writer

Durham police and public officials paid tribute to North Carolina law enforcement officers killed in the line of duty during a Peace Officers' Memorial Day service Friday.

The noon ceremony at police headquarters marked the beginning of North Carolina Law Enforcement Officers' week and set the stage for a statewide memorial service to be held at the State Capitol on Monday.

State Attorney General Lacy H. Thornburg was the guest speaker at the ceremony, which was capped with a 21-gun salute by the Durham Police Honor Guard and the playing of taps by Durham Police Cpl. Bonney G. Earp.

During his speech, Thornburg told the 50 or more people attending the service that law enforcement officers deserve the support and respect of every citizen.

"In our society, there is no higher calling than that of a call to public service," he said.

The families of officers killed in the line of duty also deserve the respect and honor of all citizens, Thornburg said.

When a law enforcement officer is killed, "it is the law enforcement officers' families that suffer most of all," he said.

Durham Mayor Wib Gulley said it is very appropriate for the community to pause and reflect on the job of the men and women in law enforcement.

"It is no small task that the men and women that serve perform," Gulley said.

Durham Police Chief Trevor A. Hampton said law enforcement work is difficult and that police are constantly scrutinized and criticized.

"We recognize that as a part of our job and we accept that," he

See **Tribute/3C**

Durham Morning Herald/Rick Sorenson

Officers prepare to fire 21-gun salute in honor of lawmen killed in line of duty